Speaking the Truth in Love to Muslims

Roland Cap Ehlke

NORTHWESTERN PUBLISHING HOUSE
Milwaukee, Wisconsin

Dedicated to Lori,
Rich, Cari, Joshua

Library of Congress Control Number: 2003111426
Northwestern Publishing House
1250 N. 113th St., Milwaukee, WI 53226-3284
© 2004 by Northwestern Publishing House
www.nph.net
Published 2004
Printed in the United States of America
ISBN 0-8100-1592-7

Contents

Maps

Photographs

Illustrations

Introduction

Then we will no longer be infants, tossed back and
forth by the waves, and blown here and there
by every wind of teaching and by the cunning and
craftiness of men in their deceitful scheming.
Instead, speaking the truth in love, we will in all
things grow up into him who is the Head, that is,
Christ. (Ephesians 4:14,15)

For Americans and much of the world, September 11,
2001, is a day never to be forgotten. As with no previous
event, including the attack on Pearl Harbor, 9-11 brought
home the reality that terrorism can—and, indeed, has—come
to mainland America. More than that, together with wars in
Iraq and Afghanistan, it has thrust into national conscious-
ness the reality of a world religion that in the past has often
been ignored and overlooked by much of the Western world.
That religion, of course, is Islam.

It may surprise many to learn that Islam has a long-standing
relationship with lands where Christianity flourishes. In fact,
for almost 14 centuries, the Christian-Muslim encounter has
been at the center of much of world history. Spread over two

centuries and costing untold lives, the Crusades are a prime example of how bloody the encounter has been at times. Recent events demonstrate that the antagonism still runs deep. On the other hand, in our relativistic and ecumenical age, there is often a tendency to see all religions as essentially the same and, as far as many are concerned, certainly not worth fighting over or even arguing about.

The "war on terrorism" may ebb and flow, but the presence of Islam remains an ongoing challenge to Christians. With well over one billion followers, Islam today is second in numbers only to the combined branches of Christianity. Together, the two religions account for some three billion followers, half of the world's population. And, especially with the collapse of much of atheistic communism, Islam and Christianity are the most powerful forces vying for people's hearts and minds in today's world. As we enter the third millennium of Christianity, the Christian-Muslim encounter once again looms large on the horizon.

Just how do these two faiths fit together? Are they diametrically opposed to each other? Many would tell us that Christianity and Islam are both saying pretty much the same things and that, when all is said and done, we all worship the same God. *Speaking the Truth in Love to Muslims* will examine such questions and such answers. Most significantly for Christians, we will not examine the issues on the basis of popular opinion or that of historians, politicians, and other authorities. Rather, we will look at Islam in the light of God's Word, the Bible.

Some 30 years ago, I spent a year studying at the Hebrew University in Jerusalem. During that time I lived in the old, walled city of Jerusalem and daily rubbed shoulders with Christians, Jews, and Muslims, several of whom became my friends. I also have traveled in Muslim countries: Egypt, Lebanon, Syria, Jordan, Turkey, Iran (having studied Farsi in a Peace Corps training program), Afghanistan, and Pakistan.

Over the years I have retained my interest in the Muslim faith, having studied Muslim history at the university level and having been involved in Muslim-Christian dialogue and debate. For several years I have been teaching the "World of Islam" course at Concordia University in Wisconsin, and at times have had the opportunity to introduce Christ to Muslim students. Through reading, research, and editing projects, I have tried to keep current on Islam.

Our study consists of three main sections. In the first section (chapters 1–3), we will gain some necessary background information on the Muslim religion, going back to the time of its founder, Muhammad, and tracing its spread. Then we will consider some of the basic teachings and practices of Islam (chapters 4–6). Finally, we will compare Islam with the Christian faith, focusing on how God's law and gospel apply to Muslims and how we can share the love of Jesus with our Muslim friends and neighbors (chapters 7–10).

Much information about Islam floods the news waves and pours off the presses. What can this book add that others have not already said? For one thing, this study has a Lutheran emphasis, showing that many issues we face were already addressed clearly and forcefully by Martin Luther. Moreover, while not a technical treatise, this study will give the lay reader enough of a background on Islam to understand its role in today's world. More important, it will provide a biblical approach to Islam and to sharing our faith with Muslims. Given the urgent need, there is much room for more biblically based and Christ-centered materials; I hope this examination of Islam will inspire readers to become involved in further study.

This book is not politically correct. Islam has had a tremendous impact on the world, but, spiritually, it is not a great religion. Claiming to build upon biblical truth, it denies the very center of that revelation—Jesus Christ as true God and true man, the Savior of the world. It does no one any good to gloss over the vast differences between Christianity and Islam. The point is not that Christians are better than Muslims—all people are sinners in need of a Savior. Rather, the point is that Christianity offers a Savior, while Islam merely offers more rules by which people must try to save themselves. At a time when Muslim spokesmen are flooding every channel of communication available to discredit the Bible, undermine the doctrine of the Trinity, and deny the saving work of Christ, Christians are compelled to "contend for the faith" (Jude 3) and "take . . . the sword of the Spirit, which is the word of God" (Ephesians 6:17).

To help in the study of Islam, there are maps and photos, an extensive vocabulary list gathered from numerous sources, questions for study and discussion, and a bibliography with a wide range of material from popular articles to learned works. Numerous quotations from original sources (the Qur'an, hadith, Muslim legal texts, the Bible) and from other books and articles (from the old to the very recent) allow readers to see and evaluate for themselves rather than simply through the eyes of this writer. In developing this book, I am grateful to editor Curt Jahn along with the staff at Northwestern Publishing House and to my friend Jacob, a former Muslim, whose Christian testimony has been an inspiration to many.

Amid the international upheavals, uncertainties, and tragedies of this world, God alerts us to the opportunities he gives us to impart the gospel, the good news of salvation in Jesus Christ. For 21st-century believers, one of the greatest and most promising of these opportunities is to speak the truth in love to Muslims.

Part 1.

Muslim Backgrounds

1. Muhammad and His Times

The Bible speaks of how the name of Jesus "is above every name, that at the name of Jesus every knee should bow, in heaven and on earth and under the earth" (Philippians 2:9,10). When it comes to naming children, however, it is said that throughout the world the most popular name that parents give to sons is the name Muhammad. Who was this man whose name and whose religion have spread around the globe? In this chapter, we will go back in time to the beginnings of Islam in Arabia and examine the setting in which Muhammad lived and taught. As we do so, we will pay special attention to some of the Jewish and Christian influences with which he met. Although much of Muhammad's life is shrouded in mystery, enough is known to get a picture of the man who founded Islam.

Arabic Names

Many names coming from Arabic have various English spellings. Some examples are Muhammad (Mohammed), Ka'abah (Kaaba), Madinah (Medina), Makkah (Mecca), Muslim (Moslem), Qur'an (Koran), Sura (Surah). In general, this book follows the usage of the Islamic Affairs Department of Saudi Arabia; in some cases, however, the more common terms are used, for example, Mecca and Medina rather than Makkah and Madinah.

Seventh-Century Arabia

As the seventh century after the birth of Jesus was about to dawn, the land of Arabia was a place of menacing deserts and, as one historian puts it, "severe beauty." Much of Arabia was like a sea of sand bordering the so-called Fertile Crescent, where the great civilizations of Babylon, Assyria, and Israel had flourished. The desert land of Arabia was the home of scattered oases and towns, rest stops along the way for camel caravans.

Its most colorful inhabitants were the Bedouins, or nomads, who spent their lives wandering from one grazing area to another in a constant search for water and an ongoing struggle against the heat. The word *Arab* refers to this wandering life. Within Bedouin society, several families would constitute a clan, several clans a tribe, and several tribes might join together into a confederation. Each of the many Bedouin tribes was led by a shaikh, or elder, who held to the ideals of bravery and loyalty in the group. Intertribal warfare, raiding, and blood feuds were common. So was polygamy, which was a way to increase the size of families and thus make individual tribes stronger.

According to Islam, the Arabs trace their ancestry back to Ishmael (Arabic: Ismail), the oldest son of Abraham (Ibrahim). The Bible's listing of Ishmael's sons (Genesis 25:12-18) supports this claim, as it includes a number of Arabic names. Already at the time of Jacob and his sons, the Ishmaelites were known as traders. Joseph's brothers sold him to "a caravan of Ishmaelites," who took Joseph to Egypt (Genesis 37:12-36).

The Arabs and Jews are also related linguistically. Both Hebrew and Arabic are Semitic languages, as evidenced in numerous related words, such as the words for *peace: shalom* (Hebrew) and *salaam* (Arabic). At the same time, it should be kept in mind that since there were two major Arab groupings—northern and southern—many Arabs are not descended from Ishmael (Glassé 58).

The most important artistic expression among the Arabs was poetry. "The beauty of a man," said an Arabic proverb, "lies in the eloquence of his tongue." The poet was thought to "be in league with unseen powers and could by his curses bring evil upon the enemy" (Hitti 90,94). Poetry was a means to extol the themes of love, courage, and the greatness of one's tribe or clan. Among the pre-Islamic legends is the story of the Arab warrior Anatara. Lines from one of the poems about this legendary figure capture the ideals of bravado, courage, and strength; they also describe the warrior's horse in battle:

> Praise me therefore for the things you know of
> me; for I
> am easy to get on with, provided I'm not
> wronged;

but if I am wronged, then the wrong I do
    is harsh indeed . . .

And many's the good wife's spouse I have left on
    the floor
the blood whistling from his ribs like a harelip
    hissing . . .

When I beheld the people advancing in solid mass
urging each other on, I wheeled on them
    blamelessly;
"Anatara!" they were calling, and the lances were
    like
well-ropes sinking into the breast of my black
    steed.
Continuously I charged them with his
    white-blazoned face . . .
    (Arberry, *Aspects of Islamic Civilization* 26-7)

Following the death of Muhammad, it was such Arab horse-men who would take the message of Islam throughout the Middle East, across the sands of North Africa, and to the gates of Europe.

But that would come later, for at the time of the prophet Muhammad's birth, about A.D. 570, two powerful empires lay to the north of the Arabian Peninsula. To the northwest was the Christian Byzantine Empire, with its capital in Constan-tinople (now Istanbul). To the northeast was the Sassanian or Persian Empire, whose religion of Zoroastrianism spoke of an ongoing battle between good and evil. The Byzantines and Sassanians were constantly at war, weakening each other and unknowingly preparing the way for their falls before the armies of Islam.

Religion in Arabia

Most of the people of Arabia were polytheists, that is, they worshiped many different gods. Pilgrims made annual jour-

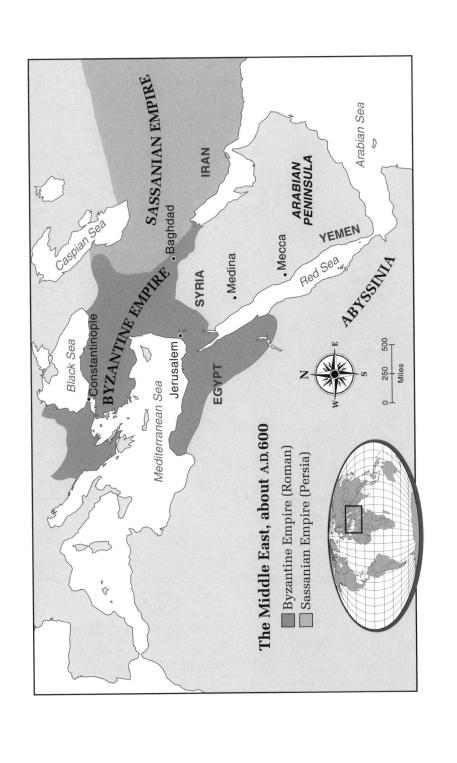

The Middle East, about A.D. 600

Byzantine Empire (Roman)
Sassanian Empire (Persia)

SASSANIAN EMPIRE

BYZANTINE EMPIRE

IRAN

Baghdad

ARABIAN PENINSULA

YEMEN

ABYSSINIA

Arabian Sea

Caspian Sea

SYRIA

Medina

Mecca

Red Sea

Black Sea

Constantinople

Jerusalem

EGYPT

Mediterranean Sea

N   E
W   S

0   250   500
Miles

neys to the pagan shrine in Mecca (Makkah), the largest city in Arabia, situated some 50 miles inland from the Red Sea. There they visited the Ka'abah, a stone edifice said to have been built by Ibrahim (Abraham) and Ismail (Ishmael). In the days of Muhammad, this structure housed the venerated Black Stone and some 360 idols representing the divinities of the Hijaz, the western part of what is now Saudi Arabia. Among the gods of Arabia was the high god known as Allah, as well as the three goddesses of Mecca: Manat, Allat, and Al-Uzza. Just as there were hundreds of deities, so there were hundreds of tribes, each with its own god.

Along with believing in many gods, the Arabs believed in jinns, demon spirits that were said to inhabit the trees, stones, rivers, and hills. The Quraysh tribe of Mecca had in its possession a black stone—probably a meteorite—that it considered to have magical power. When people came on pilgrimage to Mecca, they would kiss this stone, which was housed in the Ka'abah. This custom would carry into Islam, as would other pagan rites, such as the month of fasting based on a lunar calendar.

It was not only for religion that people went to Mecca; the pilgrimage was as much or more for trading, business, and socializing. Reading histories of the period shortly before Muhammad's birth, one gets the impression that Arabs of pre-Islamic times—referred to by Muslims as *Jahiliyya,* the "time of ignorance"—were less interested in religion than in trade, romance (with its accompanying poetry), and the almost sportsmanlike activity of intertribal raiding.

When the prophet Muhammad was born in Mecca, about the year 570, Arabia was ripe for change. Although polytheism was still the chief religion of this tribal society, it had lost its grip on many of the people and it appears that much of the religion was not deeply held. The rise of the Hanifs attests to this; these were people who rejected polytheism and believed in one supreme God.

Among those who believed in one God were the Jewish tribes. They had considerable power in Arabia, as would be shown during Muhammad's life by the ability of independent Jewish tribes to engage in battles with Arabs.

Scattered within Arabia, Christians did not wield that sort of physical might, at least not in the areas around Mecca and Medina. Nevertheless, the one million square mile Arabian Peninsula was ringed with Christian influences. Christian populations dominated Syria to the north and Abyssinia and Egypt in Africa to the west, while they had made inroads in Yemen in southern Arabia and in Persia to the northeast.

Eastern or Byzantine Christianity had long been established in what we now refer to as the Middle East. Three centuries had passed since the time of the Emperor Constantine and the Edict of Milan (313), which marked the end of Roman persecution of the Christians. Christianity had been a favored religion long enough for worldliness to set in, and long enough for a reaction to worldliness in the form of monasticism. Arabs were familiar with the lonely dwellings of monks in the deserts.

Moreover, the canon of the New Testament had long been settled upon. The canon consists of those books that are divinely inspired and came to be recognized as such. While a few books—James, 2 Peter, 2 and 3 John, Jude—"were rather persistently unrecognized" (Geisler and Nix 293), by the year 367, the "Father of Orthodoxy," Athanasius, could confidently speak of the 27 canonical books of the New Testament. These inspired books dated back to the first century and were recognized as having been written within the lifetime of the apostles and eyewitnesses to Jesus. In addition to New Testament Scriptures, the books of the Old Testament, both with and without the Apocrypha (a section of books used in Roman Catholic Bibles but not in the inspired Hebrew Old Testament), had been in use among Christians and Jews alike for centuries.

By the time of Muhammad (570–632), the Bible had been translated into Syriac, Coptic, Ethiopic, Latin, Gothic, and other languages. The earliest Arabic translation, however, did not come until about 720, almost one hundred years after Muhammad's death.

Numerous non-canonical writings, most of them postdating the Bible, were also in circulation. There were the New Testament Apocrypha and Pseudepigrapha—writings that were not a part of the inspired Scriptures—and, among Jews, the Talmud, produced between the first and fifth centuries A.D.

Eastern Christendom had had its share of controversies. Arianism (the belief that Jesus was created and is not equal to God the Father) and the subsequent Trinitarian conflicts had already passed their prime, but the conflicts over the two natures in Christ had led to further splits among believers. One key term in the debates was *theotokos,* a Greek word applied to the virgin Mary as the "bearer of God." The term gave way to *mater theo,* "mother of God." In their use of such terminology, some raised their devotion to Mary to that of a cult. These people were known as Monophysite Christians, because they believed that Jesus had only one nature *(monophysis),* and they failed to recognize the biblical truth that he is true man as well as true God. This is of interest because the Christianity to which Arabs were exposed was mainly of the Monophysite persuasion.

Such controversies with their political and, at times, violent ramifications are a sad part of church history. Yet amid the misguided approaches to dealing with the issues, another factor stands out. That factor is the centrality of the person of Jesus Christ to the Christian faith. Among Christians no one disagreed that he is the central figure of Scripture, in the Old as well as the New Testament. Nor was there disagreement that he was unique among all men ever to live on this earth. Indeed, the primary documents of Christendom—that is, the canonical Scriptures—asserted that Jesus was a man and also uniquely divine, the Son of man and the Son of God. The bitter arguments arose over attempts to explain that which really surpasses explanation.

At first glance, some of this may be of little interest to 21st-century Christians. Yet it affected Islam. As we will see throughout this book, many of the ideas of Christianity that Muhammad had and that he passed on to his followers were either mistaken ideas about the Bible or heretical views that were not in the 66 inspired, canonical books of the Bible. Muhammad's conceptions would come out in the Qur'an and give countless people confusing and wrong ideas about the Bible and about Jesus.

This, then, was the political and theological climate of the Middle East on the eve of Islam. The prophet Muhammad moved in this atmosphere, was influenced by it, and incorporated it into the Qur'an and Islam.

Muhammad's Early Life

There are three basic sources for the life of Muhammad. The first is the Qur'an, which is a record of Muhammad's words to his followers. While the text is reliable in regard to what Muhammad actually said, it contains little of a biographical nature. Rather, it consists largely of moral injunctions.

A second source of information about Muhammad consists of biographies. The earliest biography comes from Muhammad ibn Ishaq, who wrote about 120 years after the prophet's death. Another early biography comes from Waqidi, who died almost 200 years after the prophet. This gap between Muhammad and his biographers is striking when we compare it with the gap between Jesus and his four biographers, the gospel writers Matthew, Mark, Luke, and John. Each one of them was a contemporary of Jesus; in fact, two of them (Matthew and John) were among his 12 disciples. Their writings were finished within the first generation of Christians.

The hadith comprise the third source of information about Muhammad. These are the traditions that sprang up about Muhammad after his death and were passed down from one generation to the next. The examination of which hadith are more accurate has been a consuming study of Islamic scholars to this day.

The many histories of Muhammad that have come down through the ages are all based on these three sources.

Little is known of the prophet's early years. He was born around the year 570 to the ruling tribe in Mecca, the Quraysh. As noted previously, the Arabian tribes were broken into subgroups, known as clans; Muhammad was of the Hashim clan. His full name is Muhammad b. Abd Allah, that is, Muhammad the son (*b.* is short for *ibn,* which means "son") of Abd Allah (Servant of Allah).

As a child he was orphaned and raised by an uncle, Abu Talib. Muhammad spent several years among the Bedouins in the desert, where he became involved in tending sheep and goats in the hills and valleys around Mecca. There he developed a love for the rich Arabic language that was the Bedouins' proudest art. The melodious sound of the Qur'an in Arabic probably owes much to these early experiences of the prophet.

The young Muhammad also traveled with trade caravans. On these journeys he went as far as Palestine, Syria, and Yemen (see map on page 9). No doubt he came into contact with Christians and Jews at this time. Muslim tradition says that on one trip with his uncle, the young Muhammad met a Syrian monk named Bahira, who pronounced to Abu Talib, "Something very great will happen to this nephew of yours" (Ibn Ishaq 24).

At the age of 25, Muhammad began working for a woman named Khadija, who enlisted him to take charge of a caravan of hers that was to go to Syria. Khadija was a widow 15 years older than Muhammad. That she managed her own caravan

14

trade attests to her wealth and business acumen. Apparently Muhammad did well on the venture. According to Ibn Ishaq, Khadija "was an intelligent, noble and good woman." She sent for Muhammad and said to him, "O son of my uncle! I have taken a liking to you on account of our relationship, your respectability among the people, your honesty, character and veracity" (Ibn Ishaq 26). Khadija then added a proposal of marriage, which Muhammad accepted.

Muhammad's marriage to Khadija is significant for several reasons. The way in which it came about tells us something about the prophet. He was a reliable young man and was also known as quiet and thoughtful. That Khadija proposed to Muhammad is evidence of this. Moreover, Muhammad's marriage to the wealthy Khadija freed him to indulge his pensive nature. Although he remained in the caravan business for several years, Muhammad was able to devote more time to meditation and reflection. "Every year," says Ibn Ishaq, "the apostle of Allah spent a month praying at [Mount] Hira during the month of Ramadan" (36).

Muhammad and the Origin of Islam

In 610, while engaged in meditation in a desert cave in Hira near Mecca, Muhammad received what is referred to as "the call." There he heard a voice telling him, "Read!" Muhammad responded, "I cannot read." Upon the third repetition of this exchange, he said, "What can I read?" The answer was the beginning of the revelations that were to form the Qur'an, which means "the reading":

> Read: In the name of thy Lord
> Who created,
> Created man from a clot.
> Read: And it is thy Lord the most bountiful
> Who taught by the pen,
> Taught man that which he knew not. (Sura 96:1-4)

15

(Unless indicated otherwise, translations of the Qur'an are from Muhammad Marmaduke Pickthall; numbers indicate the chapter [sura] and verses.)

Muhammad's faithful wife Khadija accepted his revelation and became his first and most loyal convert. When her troubled husband returned home and told her of this experience, she said, "Rejoice, O son of my uncle . . . you will be the Prophet of this People" (Glubb 86). In contrast to the polytheism of his fellow Arabs, Muhammad began to teach a strict monotheism, devoted to the deity Allah. The name of this new religion became Islam, which means "submission" (to the will of Allah), and his followers became known as Muslims, "those who submit."

For three years, Muhammad shared his messages in private with people close to him. After that he went public. As might be expected, not everyone in Mecca was receptive to Muhammad's revelations, which he claimed came from the angel Gabriel. Some of the fiercest opposition to Muhammad developed among the wealthy Umayyah clan, which was another branch of his own tribe, the Quraysh. Initially, opposition came especially in the forms of ridicule, sneers, and sarcasm. As the revelations continued and the little band of followers grew, the reactions did too. Some of the lowlier Muslims were even beaten. In 615, Muhammad sent most of his followers—83 of them—to the largely Christian country of Abyssinia (Ethiopia) for refuge.

When Muhammad was 50 years old, his beloved wife Khadija died. As long as she had been alive, he had taken no other wives. Two months after her death, he married a second time. By the end of his life, he had married a total of 12 women.

In 622, three years after Khadija's death, the prophet himself left Mecca and emigrated to the oasis city of Yathrib (now known as Madinah, or Medina), about 250 miles north of Mecca, measured in those times as "eleven camel days north of

Mecca" (Lings 7). This migration is the famous hijirah that marks the beginning of the Islamic dating system. (Since the Muslim calendar is lunar, we cannot arrive at the Muslim year simply by subtracting 622 from the year on our calendar. Many books on Islam refer to events with both dating systems.)

At Medina, Muhammad was able to unite two large tribes that had been fighting each other. He told them that he would negotiate between them, if they agreed to accept his new religion. This diplomacy was successful and thus consolidated 80 percent of Medina behind Muhammad. It also marked the beginning of the concept of *umma*—community that crossed bloodlines and brought people together on the basis of religion.

During his years in Medina, Muhammad grew in power and took on more aggressive characteristics. His appearance was that of a dynamic leader:

> Muhammad was somewhat above middle height, with a lean but commanding figure. His head was massive, with a broad and noble forehead. He had thick black hair, slightly curling, which hung over his ears; his eyes were large black and piercing; his eyebrows arched and joined, his nose high and aquiline; and he had a long bushy beard. When he was excited, his veins would swell across his forehead. His eyes were often bloodshot and always restless. Decision marked his every movement. He used to walk so rapidly that his followers half-ran behind him and could hardly keep up with him. (Shorrosh 50)

During the first year in their new city, the Muslims built a mosque, their place of worship, as well as houses for themselves. Muhammad also took a third wife, Aisha, who was the daughter of his best friend, Abu Bakr, and to whom he had been engaged since she was six years old. At the time of their marriage, she was nine.

17

Muhammad's followers began to intercept caravans as a means of putting pressure on his enemies in Mecca. At the Battle of Badr, Muhammad, together with about three hundred followers, attacked a caravan headed to Mecca. In defeating a force of one thousand men, Muhammad gained his first military victory. When the head of the enemy leader was thrown at Muhammad's feet, Muhammad is said to have declared, "It is more acceptable to me than the choicest camel in Arabia" (Shorrosh 58). Badr was an immense turning point in Muslim history. Although he would meet with some setbacks, such as the disastrous battle at Uhud, Muhammad continued to increase in power.

His victories included the capture and near-extermination of the Jewish banu-Qurayzah tribe, which had made the mistake of siding with the prophet's Meccan enemies. In the marketplace of Medina, the Muslims decapitated hundreds of the men of this tribe, a process that lasted into the night as "the last to die were beheaded by torchlight" (Lings 232). "In number," writes Ibn Ishaq, "[the dead] amounted to six or seven hundred, although some state it to have been eight or nine hundred" (129).

Interestingly, the same man who led and planned dozens of battles and oversaw the beheading of his enemies was also known to have a gentle side. He lived in relative simplicity, mended his own clothes, and, as Aisha said, "laughed often and smiled much" (Shorrosh 50).

One of the most famous stories from Muhammad's life is that of his "night journey" *(isra)*. The report is based on one verse from the Qur'an: "Glorified be He Who carried His servant by night from the Inviolable Place of Worship [Mecca] to the Far Distant Place of Worship [Jerusalem] the neighborhood whereof we have blessed, that We might show him of our tokens [signs]" (Sura 17:1). Tradition has added the detail that the prophet journeyed through the air on the winged horse al-Buraq. From Jerusalem, Muhammad, accompanied by the angel Jibril (Gabriel), is said to have ascended (the *miraj*) through seven heavens and to have entered God's presence (Sura 53:13-8). Then he returned to Arabia, all within one night (some say within the time of a knock on the door of his house)!

This story has huge implications. The Muslim Dome of the Rock in Jerusalem is believed to mark the site, making Jerusalem the most important Muslim place next to Mecca and Medina. The mount where the Dome stands along with the al-Aqsa mosque (literally, "the furthest place of worship") is Mount Moriah, where the temple in Jerusalem once stood; so it is a holy place for Jews as well as Muslims.

On a more earthly plane, by the year 629, Muhammad's power was such that he was able to return from Medina to Mecca and take it without opposition. He proceeded to destroy the idols of the Ka'abah, and the inhabitants of Mecca embraced Islam.

Having established himself as master of much of Arabia and having unified its many tribes under Islam, the prophet died in Medina in the year 632.

The last ten years of the prophet's life were more than years of military conquest. Muhammad's decade in Medina was formative for the Muslim religion. It was during those years that he composed much of the Qur'an. One scholar sums up the importance of that final period: "Islam as it finally took shape belongs to Medina and not to Mecca" (Bell 125).

Later chapters will compare the life, ministries, and teachings of Muhammad with those of Jesus.

2. Islam's Glorious Past

Beginning in Jerusalem on the day of Pentecost, the Christian faith spread through the preaching of the gospel, the good news of salvation in Jesus Christ. The book of Acts tells how, despite persecutions, the first Christians "preached the word wherever they went" (Acts 8:4). During the first three centuries of its existence, the Christian church suffered persecutions—at times intensely—and at other times enjoyed some relief. In the words of the church father Tertullian (160–240), "Blood of the martyrs is the seed of the church." Not until the reign of the Roman Emperor Constantine (306–337) did Christianity become an accepted religion, indeed, the favored religion of the Roman Empire.

The early centuries of Islam followed a much different pattern. Already during the lifetime of Muhammad, his religion spread by means of the sword. At the time of his death, the prophet was ruler over most of Arabia.

That pattern of conquest did not stop with his passing. When Muhammad died in the arms of his favorite wife, Aisha, he had not yet clearly picked a successor. There is some indication in the traditions that he had favored his cousin and son-in-law Ali bin Abi Talib, but the matter of the prophet's successor would become a cause of strife that would forever divide Muslims.

Much of what we hear about Islam today is closely related to its history. This chapter will review some of the key features of Islamic history, which will help in understanding why so many Muslims around the world long for Islam's glorious past.

Some Key Dates in Muslim History:

570–632	The life of the prophet Muhammad
622	The flight to Medina, marking the beginning of the Muslim calendar
638	Muslims conquer Jerusalem
680	Husain, grandson of Muhammad, killed at Karbala, split between Sunnis and Shiites
732	Islamic forces stopped at battle of Tours in France
1095	Pope Urban II calls for crusade, beginning of 200 years of the Crusades
1453	Ottoman Turks take Constantinople (Istanbul), threaten Europe from the east
1492	Fall of Granada, Moors (Spanish Muslims) driven from Spain
1699	Ottoman expansion stopped, beginning of long decline
1798	Napoleon in Egypt, battle of the Pyramids
1803	Wahabis capture Mecca and Medina
1924	Caliphate abolished following fall of Ottoman Empire
1948	Israel proclaims independence
2001	September 11th terrorist attacks on United States

The Spread of Islam under the Rightly Guided Caliphs

The early and formative history of Islam revolves around the first four successors of Muhammad, all of whom ruled from the city of Medina in Arabia. They each took the title of caliph *(khalifa)*, which means "successor," "deputy," or "substitute," and for centuries this was the designation of the leader of the Muslim community. The first four successors have become known as the "Rightly Guided Caliphs," since they personally knew and heard Muhammad and were guided by his living example. Subsequent to their periods of leadership, Islam would break into diverse parties.

Abu Bakr was the first caliph. The father of Muhammad's wife Aisha and one of the first converts to Islam, Abu Bakr had accompanied the prophet on the hijirah from Mecca to Medina. When Muhammad died rather unexpectedly on June 8, 632, after a short illness, some thought that the successor might be the prophet's "proud and handsome" cousin and son-in-law Ali (Payne 88). But it was Abu Bakr and his contingency that held sway while Ali was absent from the scene. The very evening of the prophet's death, Abu Bakr became his successor.

After only two years as caliph, Abu Bakr died at the age of 63. One historian has summed up the rule of Abu Bakr with these positive words: "He was the greatest of the Caliphs, the most generous, the most devout, the most learned," writes Robert Payne. "None of his successors believed so firmly in the goodness of God, and none was so saintly" (88). His reputation earned him the Arabic title *al-Siddiq,* "the righteous or honest one," a title given by Muslims to no one else except Joseph (*Yusuf* in the Qur'an). This is significant not only for what it says about the first caliph, but also for what it does not say about those who followed him.

Islam had been consolidated within Arabia, but during the short caliphate of Abu Bakr (632–634), it had begun to spread beyond the Arabian Peninsula. One reason for mov-

ing outside Arabia was to unite the Arab tribes, some of
which were revolting and were wanting to separate from the
others following Muhammad's death. Although the caliph
was not personally involved in the fighting, his armies
moved north into Syria.

Umar b. al-Khattab was the second caliph (634–644),
appointed by Abu Bakr on his deathbed. He was the father of
Muhammad's wife Hafsa. Like Muhammad and Abu Bakr, he
was from the Quraysh tribe. During the caliphate of this very
capable ruler, the Muslims took the cities of Damascus and
Jerusalem under the "dominant figure" of General Khalid b.
al-Walid (Guillaume 79). In addition to expanding the Islamic
empire, "Umar made his starting point the theory that in the
[Arabian] peninsula itself none but the Moslem religion
should ever be tolerated," and he proceeded to drive out Jews
and Christians (Hitti 169). Umar was stabbed to death at the
hands of a Persian slave, an omen of the internal strife that
would plague so much of Muslim history.

Before moving on to the next two caliphs, it is worthwhile
to consider some of the reasons for the extraordinary suc-
cesses of the Arab armies as they began their sweep throughout the Middle East and far beyond. It has been argued that
the controversies among Eastern Christendom left the area
wide open for Muslim conquest and conversion. But there
was something else that may have had much greater impact.
That factor was of a political rather than theological nature.
We turn to John Glubb's crisp summary of it:

> The factor, however, which, more than any other,
> was to facilitate the Muslim conquests was that, in
> 602, the King of Persia, Chrosroes Parwiz, invaded
> the Byzantine Empire. In 614, he took Damascus,
> and, in 616, he simultaneously occupied Egypt
> and all Asia Minor. Not until 628 was peace
> restored, on the basis of the frontiers of 602. After

twenty-six years of war, both of the great empires
were in a state of bankruptcy and anarchy. (54)

In addition to the exhaustion of the two powers to the
north of Arabia, other factors contributed to Muslim success.
The Arabs' use of the camel gave them both speed and mobil-
ity. Perhaps more than anything else, the Muslims were
inspired by their new religion, which promised them entrance
into paradise if they should die in battle. Unlike the
Byzantines and Persians who relied on professional, paid soldiers, every Muslim was in effect a soldier. Under Umar many
Arabs moved into the newly conquered areas, where the
people were divided into two classes: the Muslim rulers and
the non-Muslim subjects.

Uthman b. Affan became the third caliph (644–656). An
early convert to Islam, he was of the Umayyah family of the
Quraysh tribe; from this once-hostile family would come a
dynasty that would soon rule the growing Muslim empire.
"This man [Uthman]," notes Guillaume, "who had a reputation for running away from battle, was a member of one of the
ruling families of Mecca, and his appointment spelt the ruin
of the hopes of the Medinans, who had contributed everything
to the success of the prophet" (81). Uthman showed a great
deal of favoritism to his own family, a practice that aroused
much antagonism among other Muslims. Muhammad b. Abu
Bakr, son of the first caliph, led a rebellion and was involved
in the death of the 83-year-old leader, who was stabbed while
reading the Qur'an in his house in Medina.

Aside from the continued expansion of the empire by his
generals, Uthman's caliphate is noted especially for establish-
ing the Qur'an in the form in which it has come down to the
present. Prior to Uthman's time, there were several versions
of the Qur'an. According to one account, Muhammad's harsh
words against the Umayyads were removed from this
accepted text, while copies belonging to Muhammad's family

were confiscated (Payne 108). At any rate, all versions other than the official one were removed from libraries and burned.

Ali b. Abi Talib was the fourth caliph (656–661). Like Muhammad, he came from the Hashim clan of the Quraysh tribe. He was the prophet's cousin and also became the prophet's son-in-law when he married Muhammad's daughter Fatima. According to Ibn Ishaq, after the prophet's wife Khadija, Ali was the second convert to Islam (39).

From the start, however, Ali's rule was marked with strife. He was involved in battles against other early followers and relatives of the prophet, including Muhammad's wife Aisha, who, after being defeated by the forces of Ali in the Battle of the Camel at Basra, spent the last 12 years of her life in Medina. Ali's claim to the caliphate was contested by Muawiya, the founder of the Umayyad dynasty. Ali met his death by being stabbed in the brain by a poisoned sword at the hands of a Kharijite, a member of a group who accepted the leadership of neither Ali nor his rival Muawiya. Ironically, as will become clear shortly, in his death Ali became more renowned and influential than he had been in life.

With the death of Ali, the early formative period of the four "Rightly Guided Caliphs" came to an end. That designation sets them apart from the more secular rulers of the two great dynasties to follow: the Umayyads and the Abbasids.

Early Islamic Empires: The Umayyads and the Abbasids

The *Umayyad* dynasty was to last almost a century, from 661 to 750. With the caliphate of Muawiya, the capital of the Muslim world moved from Medina in Arabia to Damascus in Syria, and in the years following, other momentous changes would take place in the world of Islam.

In spite of internal hostilities, even civil war, the Muslim empire continued to expand. This territory would become known as the *dar al-Islam,* "the house of Islam"—the territory under Islamic sovereignty or the areas where Islam was secure—and it stands in contrast to the *dar al-harb,* "the abode of war"—the territory not under Muslim sovereignty, against which warfare for the propagation of Islam was considered acceptable.

During the Umayyad period, Muslim armies adopted more conventional forms of fighting and continued to expand across North Africa and through Spain in the west and to India in the east. The Muslims also became a naval power and invaded and captured the island of Sicily, from which they were able to raid the mainland and threaten the city of Rome itself.

Meanwhile, the internal strife continued. Ali's oldest son, Hasan, abdicated the caliphate to Muawiya and then retired with his 60 wives to Medina where he was poisoned. In 680, Ali's younger son, Husain, was killed at the Battle of Karbala in Iraq. This historic event created an immense rift in the world of Islam. The followers of Ali's family became known as the Shiites (the Arabic word *shi'a* means "party," that is, the party of Ali). This is the largest minority group in Islam (the majority are known as Sunnis), concentrated mainly in Iran and southern Iraq. Ali and Husain, who is known to Shiites as the "Prince of the Martyrs," are venerated and their burial places are considered holy sites and places of pilgrimages.

During the Umayyad Empire, the mosque took on a new prominence not only as a place of worship, but also as a display of artistic excellence. In the capital, a Christian church was converted into the beautiful Damascus Mosque. But the oldest and most famous example of early Islamic art and architecture is the Dome of the Rock (691) in Jerusalem (see the photo on page 29). Because of the Muslim injunction against representing human images, calligraphy became an art form unto itself with selections from the Qur'an in Arabic surrounding the building, which is located on Mount Moriah, where the Jewish temples once stood. According to Muslim tradition, Muhammad experienced a miraculous night jour-

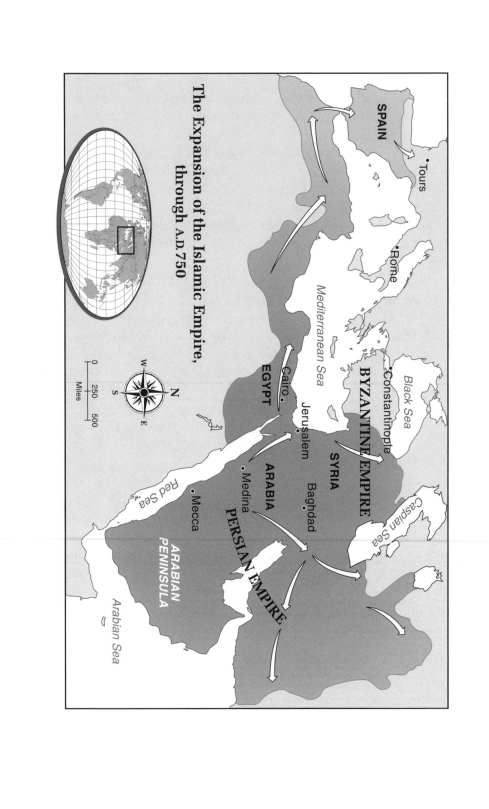

The Expansion of the Islamic Empire, through A.D.750

SPAIN

Tours

Rome

Mediterranean Sea

Constantinople

Black Sea

BYZANTINE EMPIRE

EGYPT

Cairo

Jerusalem

SYRIA

Baghdad

Caspian Sea

ARABIA

Medina

PERSIAN EMPIRE

Mecca

Red Sea

ARABIAN PENINSULA

Arabian Sea

N
W   E
S

0
250
500
Miles

© CORBIS

The Dome of the Rock, Jerusalem

ney to paradise at this site, and it is now the most holy place in Islam next to Medina and Mecca.

Under the Umayyads, Muslim armies marched through Spain and into France. Finally, at the Battle of Tours (or Poitiers) in northwestern France, Muslim forces were met and stopped by Charles Martel ("the Hammer"). Only a century after Muhammad's death, Islam now held sway over an empire that matched and even surpassed the great kingdoms of the past—including the Greeks under Alexander the Great and the Romans.

The Umayyad rulers, however, had a reputation for luxury, indulgence, and opulence. They were widely known to be more interested in politics than in piety and more concerned about being kings than caliphs. One ruler, for example, is said to have swum in a pool of wine and to have drunk enough of it to significantly lower the level. Such worldliness led to much resentment and eventually contributed to the downfall of the Umayyads.

That downfall came at the hands of the *Abbasids* (750–1258), who destroyed the last of the Umayyad rulers. Under the Abbasid dynasty, the center of Muslim power shifted eastward to the city of Baghdad, which was founded as the capital on the Tigris River in 762. The 500 years of Abbasid power marked the golden age of Muslim civilization.

This period saw the development of Muslim mysticism (Sufism, a topic for the next chapter), as well as the four chief schools of law that direct Sunni Muslim life to this day. The Abbasid era marked the zenith of Muslim art, science, philosophy, and literature, such as the *Rubaiyat* of Omar Khayyam and the fabled stories of Aladdin, *The Thousand and One Nights.* The so-called "arts of the loom" took on special significance. Wool, linen, cotton, and silk were used in almost every aspect of life, from the clothes people wore, to the carpets they walked on, to the drapery that covers Islam's most holy site, the Ka'abah (Bloom and Blair 81-98).

The Abbasid dynasty was also the epoch of the Crusades. In 1095, Pope Urban II called for a crusade to win back the city of Jerusalem from Muslim control. This set off two hundred years of intermittent warfare between Christian Europe and Islam. Four years after Urban's appeal, the crusaders captured Jerusalem. From the Crusades came the stories of bigger-than-life characters such as Richard the Lionhearted and Saladin, who retook Jerusalem for the Muslims in 1188. It was during the time of the Crusades that St. Francis of Assisi went to Egypt to try to convert the ruler there.

Interestingly, the Crusades contributed to European expansion and the modern world. As the crusaders came into contact with Middle Eastern culture, many developed a taste for the spices, silks, and other Eastern luxuries. Thwarted in their ability to travel overland through Muslim territories, Europe sought alternate ways to travel—sea routes. This indirectly led to the European discovery of the Americas. As for the morality of the Crusades, that is a subject that will be discussed in chapter 7.

Even as the Abbasid Empire flourished, there were Muslim rivals. Notable among them were the Fatimids in Egypt and the Umayyads in Spain. Founded in 963, the Egyptian city of Cairo would eventually eclipse Baghdad as the cultural, economic, and religious center of the Arabic-speaking world. In Spain, the Moors were finally expelled completely in 1492, the same year King Ferdinand and Queen Isabella commissioned Columbus on his famous voyage across the Atlantic.

The last Abbasid caliph was murdered by the Mongols, who came to power in the East under Genghis Khan, swept across Asia, and sacked the city of Baghdad. While the Abbasid period was a golden age for Islamic civilization, there was a growing tendency toward fragmentation. Several caliphates existed simultaneously and numerous dynasties arose in Spain, North Africa, Egypt, and elsewhere.

The "Gunpowder Empires": Safavids, Mughals, and Ottomans

Although it is beyond the scope of this book to trace the history of Islam in all its complexity, it is important to touch on the major periods and empires. In the centuries following the fall of the Abbasids, three powerful empires arose that were to play important roles in Muslim and world history. Although Muslim, these empires differed from the early empires in that they did not have Arab roots. They are sometimes called the "Gunpowder Empires" because they effectively used that newly developed military weapon.

The *Safavid* dynasty ruled in Persia (Iran) from 1501 to 1732. During the time of this empire, Shiism became the unifying religion of Iran. Under Shah (the title of the king) Abbas I, this empire reached its zenith, as evidenced in the art and architecture of the capital city of Isfahan. After its flowering, the empire sank into a long period of decay under the pressure of Afghan tribesmen from the east and the Ottoman Turks from the west.

The *Mughals* (a variation of the term Mongols) flourished in India from about 1526 to 1858. This empire is noteworthy for several reasons. From this region arose a synthesis of Islam and Hinduism, the chief religion of India. Moreover, the Mughals are known for their artwork, the most famous example of which is the Taj Mahal in Agra, India (see photo). Shah Jahan built this marble work of art as a monument to his wife, Mumtaz Mahal, who died while giving birth to her 13th child and beside whom he is buried within the structure. As the Mughals declined in power, the British gradually took control of India.

© Joe McDonald/CORBIS

The Taj Mahal, India

The *Ottoman* Turkish Empire (1281–1924) was the longest-lived and greatest of the Gunpowder Empires, with a legacy that continues to have a profound influence on the world today. For several centuries, the Turks had moved across the steppes of Asia, where they had absorbed the Muslim religion, and through Asia Minor, where they had gradually captured territories closer and closer to Constantinople (present-day Istanbul), the capital of the Byzantine Empire and the easternmost metropolis of Europe.

After having taken land around the city, in 1453, the Turkish Muslims took the city itself. The fall of Constantinople was an enormous catastrophe for Europe, as it brought to an end over one thousand years of the city standing as the stronghold of eastern (Orthodox) Christianity. Much of the strength of the Turkish armies came from the famous Janissaries—youths recruited from the Christian population, converted to Islam, and trained as soldiers. As the Muslims had entered

The Skyline of Istanbul, Turkey

33

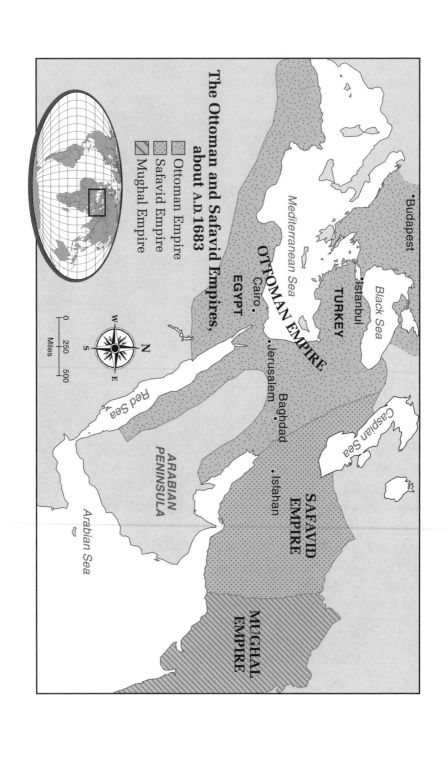

The Ottoman and Safavid Empires,
about A.D. 1683

☐ Ottoman Empire
☐ Safavid Empire
▨ Mughal Empire

0   250   500
Miles

N W E S

OTTOMAN EMPIRE

Mediterranean Sea

Budapest

Istanbul

Black Sea

TURKEY

Cairo
EGYPT

Jerusalem

Baghdad

Caspian Sea

Isfahan

Red Sea

ARABIAN
PENINSULA

**SAFAVID
EMPIRE**

Arabian Sea

**MUGHAL
EMPIRE**

Europe from the west during the time of the Umayyads, under the Ottoman Turks they would reach deep into Europe from the east, twice threatening the city of Vienna.

Dominated by the silhouettes of its mosques, Istanbul symbolized the power of Islam (see photo on p. 33). Far from its humble origins in Mecca, the Muslim faith challenged to overrun Europe, the very heart of the Christian church.

Luther and the Muslims

Lutheran history has long connections with Islam. Thirty years before Martin Luther (1483–1546) was born, Constantinople had fallen to the Ottoman Turks. Under the rule of Sultan Suleyman I the Magnificent (reigned 1520–1566), Ottoman power reached its zenith. In 1520, three years after Luther posted his Ninety-five Theses in Wittenberg, the Turks captured Belgrade; and in 1521, when Luther made his famous stand before the Emperor Charles V at Worms, they took the island of Rhodes.

In 1526, at the battle of Mohacs on the Danube River, King Louis II of Hungary fell along with 20,000 of his troops. In 1529, the army of Suleyman moved even farther into Europe and besieged the city of Vienna. Writings flooded Europe with warnings of Turkish terrors. Some called for a crusade; others urged giving up and accepting Turkish rule. Luther wrote a short book entitled *On War Against the Turk.* In it he urged Emperor Charles V to defend his subjects, who were under attack from the Turks. Luther pointed out that Islam included "much glorification of the sword" (176); he called for prayer and outlined a number of Muslim doctrines that contradicted the Bible. At the same time, he described what the duty of the emperor was—and what it was not: "The emperor should seek nothing else than simply to perform the work and duty of his office, which is to protect his subjects. . . . The emperor is not the head of Christendom or defender of the gospel or the faith" (185).

The Muslims were unable to take Vienna, but in 1541, Sultan Suleyman conquered Hungary and once again threatened Vienna along with the German lands lying beyond it. In his *Appeal for Prayer Against the Turks, 1541,* Luther spoke of the Turk as "our 'schoolmaster.' He has to discipline and teach us to fear God and to pray. Otherwise we will do what we have been doing—rot in sin and complacency" (224). Luther called upon Christians to pray for the government and for "those who are bearing the brunt of battle" (231) against the Turks who are "Satan's army" (237) and who had put Muhammad in the place of the Lord Jesus Christ. He went on to point out that the war against the Turks was a just war. He reminded Christians not to put their faith in human cleverness or might but rather to commit everything to God and not give way to fear.

In addition to these two treatises, Luther had other involvement with Islam. In 1542, he translated from Latin into German a critique of the Qur'an that had been written in 1300 by Brother Richard (Riccoldo da Montecroce), a preacher of the Dominican Order. In the forward to his translation, Luther explained the purpose for his efforts: "This way we Germans will know what an abominable religion Muhammad's belief is, and we will be strengthened in our Christian faith" (Montecroce 2). This work has recently become available in English under the title *Islam in the Crucible.*

Luther's Reformation hymn "Lord, Keep Us Steadfast in Thy Word" (1543) was originally entitled "A children's hymn, to be sung against the two archenemies of Christ and His holy Church, the Pope and the Turk." An English translation has the opening verse say:

> Lord, keep us steadfast in Thy Word;
> Curb those who fain by craft and sword
> Would wrest the Kingdom from Thy Son
> And set at naught all He hath done.
>
> (*The Lutheran Hymnal* 261:1)

In Luther's original German, the second line calls on God to "put a stop to the murder by the pope and Turk" *(Und steur des papsts und Türken Mord)* (Polack 191-2). Also in 1543, Luther and his colleague Philip Melanchthon wrote an introduction to a Latin translation of the Qur'an; this was the first European edition of the Qur'an (Miller, "Love Thy Muslim Neighbor" 7). Luther wanted people to know and be able to refute "the insanity and wiles of the devil" (7).

Later chapters will examine Luther's words on Islam in more detail, but for now it is sufficient to note the acute awareness Luther and the people of his day had of the Muslim Turks. It is an awareness that in several ways parallels our world today.

Muslim Decline and Revival

With the European discovery of the New World, along with the Renaissance, the Reformation, and the rise of modern science, Christian Europe emerged from the Middle Ages and entered the modern world. This same period marked a decline in Muslim countries. That decline was most marked in the once-dominating Ottoman Empire.

In the late 1600s, the Turks suffered several military setbacks. Then came two long centuries of decline. By the end of the 19th century, Turkey was considered the "sick man" of Europe as other countries eagerly looked forward to taking shares of what had been the Ottoman Empire. One of the causes of World War I was the assassination of Archduke Ferdinand and his wife in Sarajevo, which happened as Serbians and other nationalists tried to free themselves from Ottoman domination while European powers vied to take control.

The final blow came when Turkey sided with Germany in World War I . . . and lost. In the Middle East, Arabs fought beside the legendary British officer Lawrence of Arabia to throw off the Turks. This brought an end to the rule of the sultan and the caliphate. Following the war, the Empire was divided into what is now the Middle East. New borders were drawn and new countries, such as present-day Iraq, were formed. Among the many momentous events was the Balfour Declaration of 1917, in which the British declared that the Jews could have a home in Palestine.

For a period of some 150 years, from about 1800 to 1950, Muslim lands were dominated by European colonial powers. The French invasion of Egypt in 1798 and Napoleon's victory at the Battle of the Pyramids symbolized European domination. The creation of the state of Israel in 1948 was especially irksome as it marked the establishment of a non-Muslim nation in the dar al-Islam, the house of Islam. The once glorious Muslim empires seemed little more than desert wastelands, divided by foreigners and unbelievers. Understandably, Muslims longed for the power and prestige they had once enjoyed.

With the discovery and drilling of oil in the Middle East, Islamic hope revived. Especially within the last half century, Islam has again become a major force in the world. High birth rates and worldwide expansion make Islam the world's fastest growing religion. And many Muslims are willing to lay down their lives to fight and destroy the enemies of Islam. The glories of the past are the dreams for tomorrow.

3. The Mosaic of Islam Today

At times Muslims point to the many denominations of Christianity and contrast that with the unity of Islam. The fact is that Islam too is divided into many factions. In the last chapter, some of the political differences came to light. This chapter will examine religious differences among Muslims.

It might be expected that a religion as old and as large as Islam would have its share of divisions, and that is just the case. Islam is divided into two major sects with numerous subgroups, as well as some offshoots that have become independent world religions in their own rights.

The Major Sects: Sunnis

The vast majority (about 85 percent) of Muslims are *Sunnis.* The word *Sunni* refers to someone who adheres to the *sunna,* that is, the path or the customary practices of the prophet Muhammad. At times the word is translated as "orthodox."

According to the Sunnis, no one could match Muhammad, who was the Seal of the Prophets, the last and the greatest of the prophets. Consequently, his successors could be no more

The Family of Muhammad

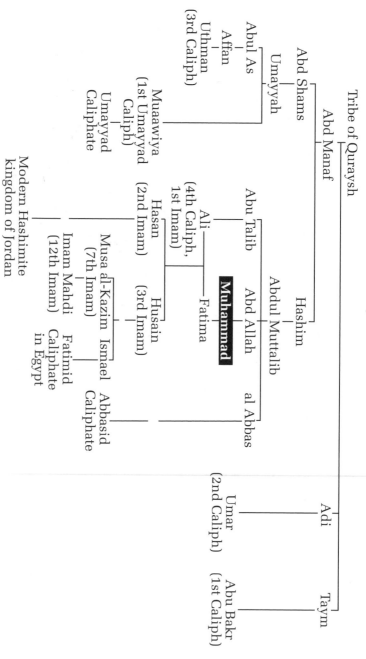

Tribe of Quraysh

Abd Manaf

- Abd Shams — Umayyah
  - Abul As — Affan — Uthman (3rd Caliph)
  - Muaawiya (1st Umayyad Caliph) — Umayyad Caliphate
- Hashim — Abdul Muttalib
  - Abu Talib
    - Ali (4th Caliph, 1st Imam) — Fatima
      - Hasan (2nd Imam)
      - Husain (3rd Imam)
        - Musa al-Kazim (7th Imam) — Imam Mahdi (12th Imam)
        - Ismael — Fatimid Caliphate in Egypt
    - Muhammad
  - Abd Allah
  - al Abbas — Abbasid Caliphate

Modern Hashimite kingdom of Jordan

- Adi — Umar (2nd Caliph)
- Taym — Abu Bakr (1st Caliph)

40

than guardians of the faith. Until the fall of the Ottoman Empire and the abolition of the caliphate in 1924, the caliph was considered that guardian.

Along with the caliphate, there have been other even more important factors that have held together Sunni Islam. One of them has been the recognition of four sources of religious authority. The primary source is the Qur'an, considered as God's word given through Muhammad. Next to the Qur'an, the most important authority is the hadith. The word means "something new," or the "news." The hadith are the traditions of what Muhammad did or said outside of the Qur'an; they contain little direct information of the prophet's life and deeds. For situations that are not covered in the Qur'an and the hadith, there are two other sources. One is reasoning (qiyas), and the other is juristic opinion (rayi), which has in the course of time been replaced by consensus of jurists' opinions (ijma').

These four sources combine to determine the shari'ah (sharia), which is considered the will of God, as expressed in the religious laws of Islam. Leaders of the ulama'—the group of scholars trained in religious law—interpret the shari'ah for the rest of the people. Sunnis believe that their leaders should be elected by consensus (ijma'), or community.

In addition to the four sources of law, another cohesive feature in Sunni Islam has been the four orthodox schools of law. Each of these legal systems was developed by or named after a noted Muslim jurist who was active during the Abbasid period. The four schools are the Maliki, Shafii, Hanafi, and Hanbali.

Each of the four schools has become influential in various Muslim lands. The Hanafi school, which is the largest and in some ways the most liberal, is prevalent in most of Turkey, India, Pakistan, and the roughly third of Iraq that is Sunni. By contrast, the Hanbali school is the most orthodox, or conservative. The Hanbalis emphasize the Qur'an and the hadith—in other words, tradition over the use of reason. Although influential elsewhere (for example, in the Bath [also spelled

41

Ba'th, Ba'ath] Party, the political party of Saddam Hussein), the Hanbali school has been adopted only in Saudi Arabia, the birthplace of Islam, which is now known as perhaps the most restrictive country on earth.

Sunni life, then, revolves around laws. The four sources set forth the many laws that govern every aspect of behavior, while the four schools interpret and apply them.

The Major Sects: Shiites

Besides the Sunnis, millions of people are found in numerous other Muslim groups. Next to the Sunnis, the largest single group is that of the *Shiites* (about 12 percent of all Muslims). The word *Shiite* comes from the Arabic word *shi'a,* which means "party." It refers to those Muslims who are of the party of Ali, that is, those who follow his claims and those of his son Husain.

The Shiites trace their origin back to Muhammad's son-in-law, Ali (died 661), and since the time of Ali have differed with the Sunnis over the spiritual leadership of Islam. In Shiite doctrine, the spiritual leader of Islam is known as the *imam,* who is from the family of the prophet and is designated by the previous imam as the successor. After the Battle of Karbala (681), Shiites developed a doctrine of redemption, according to which the imam is considered the redeemer. Ali's son Husain, who died at Karbala, is said to have died for the sins of the people; he and subsequent imams are considered saviors. The terrible massacre of Husain—his head was cut off and his body was trampled by horses—is recalled with great emotion.

The imam is not considered divine, but he is said to be infallible. Whoever was the current imam was called the Imam of the Time and became the Living Qur'an. He alone could interpret the Qur'an and all new legislation was to come from him. As such, like Muhammad (and the prophets before him), he is not a law follower but a law creator.

Rather than following the consensus of the Sunnis, the Shiites (or Shi'a) look to the authority of the imam. As one scholar has put it, "Sunni Islam is a religion of Ijma [consensus], Shia Islam a religion of authority" (Rahman 173). Among other differences between Sunnis and Shiites is that the latter permit the practice of *muta,* "temporary marriage." This means that Muslims can contract marriage for a specific period of years or even of days. Fazlur Rahman notes one other variation: "The Shi'a masses are, on the whole, more superstitious than the Sunnis" (175).

Among the Shiites there are several sects. Most Shiites are known as Twelvers because they believe in 12 imams. The last of the imams disappeared in 873, and they await the reappearance of this "hidden imam." Another Shiite group is that of the Seveners, who recognize only seven imams. They too await the reappearance of a hidden imam, although it is not the same person as that of the Twelvers. Also known as Ismailis, these Shiites await the return of an imam named Ismail, whom others reject as guilty of the sin of drinking wine. The Seveners are especially to be found in Pakistan and India.

Since the time of the Safavids (see page 31), Shiism has been the official religion of Iran, ancient Persia. The majority of people in neighboring modern Iraq are also Shiites. There, in the city of Karbala, the tomb-shrine of al-Husain b. Ali is a key site of pilgrimage, as is the tomb of Ali in Najaf, Iraq.

While Shiites and Sunnis share a common faith in Allah and the Qur'an, differences run deep. Generally they worship in separate places rather than worship together.

Islamic Mystics: Sufis

Sufism is an old movement that continues to this day. This is not a division of Islam in the same sense as is the Sunni or Shiite branch of Islam. Rather, Sufism is a movement that includes both Sunnis and Shiites. Rather than focusing on the outward manifestations of religion, the Sufis concentrate on the inward path, known as *tariqah,* "the path of love." The word *Sufi* comes from the word for *wool,* in recognition of the garments that Sufis wear.

The famous Persian poet Jalal al-Din Rumi (1207–1273) is considered the inspiration for the Sufis. Known for their asceticism and mysticism, Sufis try to attain direct encounter with God. The whirling dervishes of Turkey are Sufis who repeat the name of God as they dance, spinning around as reflections of the motions of the heavenly spheres.

Some Sufis have triggered the wrath of orthodox Islam by not only claiming to have intimate union with God but by claiming to *be* God. Many Sufis have tried to unite their adherence to Islamic law with their inward mysticism.

The following selection from Rumi is an example of Sufi poetry. The poem speaks of a reed flute (the poem is sung to the music of that instrument); yet on another level it is speaking of the soul's longing for God:

> (List[en] to the reed, how it makes its complaint,
> telling the story of its sunderings.)
> Ever since they cut me from the reed bed,
> the whole world mourns at my lament.
> I'd pierce my bosom into holes
> fully to utter the pangs of my yearning.
> One who lives far apart from his roots
> looks ever to the day of his reunion. . . .
> This lament of the reed is fire, not air;
> (may he who has not this fire be turned
>   to nothingness!).
> It is love's fire that descends into the reed; . . .
> No crudity can comprehend what ripeness is.
> Cut short this talk, and so farewell!
>
> (Levy 108)

The poem captures the Sufi's ascetic desire for freedom from the physical body and material possessions while longing to return to God, the creator.

Along with their famous poetry, the Sufis have been the most notable missionaries of Islam, bringing the faith to Indonesia, Africa, and Europe.

Other Muslim Movements

The *Ahmadiyya* Muslim movement dates from the 19th century and comes from India, but through vigorous mission activities it has made itself heard in the West. In 1889, Mirza Ghulam Ahmad, the founder of this group, pronounced himself the returned imam as well as the savior of Hinduism, Christianity, and Islam. The Ahmadiyyas claim that Jesus escaped death on the cross and eventually died in Kashmir at the age of 120. Mainstream Islam considers this group heretical, since it claims to be "the divinely prophesied revival of Islam" *(What Is Ahmadiyyat?)*.

The *Wahhabis* are Sunni followers of the austere teachings of Ibn Abd al-Wahhab (1703-1792), who lived in Arabia and came to champion a fundamental view of law as espoused by the Hanbali school. Wahhabis accept the literal authority of the Qur'an, using only words directly from the Qur'an in their daily prayers. They condemn the worship of saints and reject Sufism. They call for a strict application of the law, which includes, for instance, the cutting off of thieves' hands.

The Wahhabis' strict ideals still hold sway in Saudi Arabia. As guardians of the holy cities of Mecca and Medina, the Saudis admit no Christian missions into the country, and non-Muslims are not even allowed into Mecca or the area around the city. George Braswell notes, "Wahhabism has had deep influence upon other ultraconservative Islamic movements in worldwide Islam" (65). Among others, that influence has extended to the Taliban of Afghanistan.

Folk Islam relates to those practices of Islam that make up the everyday lives of vast numbers of Muslims. Fry and King call folk Islam the Muslim equivalent of Protestant "church suppers, and Ladies' Aid Societies," Catholic Knights of Columbus, or Jewish bar mitzvahs (87-8). Saal describes folk Islam as "a mixture of pristine Islam with the ancient religious traditions and practices of ordinary people. It exists in a world populated by angels, demons, jinn, magicians, fortune-tellers, healers, and saints (both living and dead)" (51).

In addition to the goal of making a pilgrimage to Mecca at least once in a lifetime, Muslims have other special sites, such as Karbala in Iraq, which is revered by Shiites. Dramas reenacting events from the lives of Husain and his older brother Hassan hold special meaning; and in commemoration of the death of Husain, Shiites self-flagellate their heads and chests with chains.

Muslims have also developed a reverence of Muhammad as if he were almost divine, even though he claimed to be only a man. Likewise, the birthdays of the prophet's daughter Fatima and other Muslim notaries rival the veneration paid to any saint. Shiites build shrines and pray to Ali, Husain, and others of the 12 imams. Some Muslims pray to various prophets, including Jesus. As an answer to Muslims' needs for fellowship with other believers, Muslim brotherhoods have developed, many with political interests.

When a child is born, the first words he or she hears are from the Qur'an. Although more a legal than religious matter, marriage is also attended with various pious rituals. Muslims are buried in tombs above the ground with their heads toward Mecca. In folk Islam, people who visit the tombs of Muslim saints will attain special blessing.

The *Nation of Islam* or *World Community of Islam* in the West, formerly known as the Black Muslims, began in 1930. With 50,000 members in the United States, the influence of this group is far greater than its numbers would indicate. The Nation of Islam is known for recruiting young black men and those imprisoned—like Malcolm X and Mike Tyson.

A number of its beliefs are outside historic Muslim beliefs, making this group more of a cult than a religion. For example, the Nation of Islam is polytheistic and teaches that there are many gods, including the black man: "You are walking around looking for a God to bow down to and worship. You are the God" (quoted by Buckner 8). This group believes that the black race is divine; there is no heaven or hell (to teach people to hope for heaven is said to be a way to keep slaves under control); there is no need for a Savior. According to this group's beliefs, the white race was brought into existence six thousand years ago by "a black scientist in rebellion against Allah" (Pement 7).

The Nation of Islam was founded in Detroit in 1930 by a man named Wallace D. Fard, who claimed to come from Mecca. Using borrowed Jehovah's Witness materials, Fard denied the Trinity and rejected the divinity of Jesus (Morey 163). He taught that Caucasians are "blue-eyed devils" and that Islam is the true religion for black people. When Fard disappeared in 1934, Elijah Muhammad took over. He taught that Fard had been an incarnation of Allah, a teaching that is abhorrent to mainstream Islam. The heir apparent, Malcolm X, was assassinated. At the time of this writing, Louis Farrakhan heads the group.

The Baha'is

In addition to numerous movements within the canopy of Islam, there is a major Muslim offshoot that has become a world religion in its own right: Baha'ism. According to Twelver Shiite belief, Ali had 12 descendants who were the legitimate heads of Islam. As noted above, these men were known as imams (teachers). They were also called "gates," that is, gates to the true faith. In A.D. 872, the 12th and most revered imam disappeared. Since then, Shiites have been waiting for him to return and lead them to world conquest.

In 1844, a young Persian named Mirza Ali Muhammad stepped forth and declared himself the imam and the *Bab,*

Persian for "gate." This claim set Persia on fire. In the persecutions that befell the Bab and his followers, he was executed in 1850 at the age of 30.

The Bab's religion might have died with him had it not been for one of his loyal followers, Mirza Husayn Ali. The Bab had claimed to be the last in a long line of prophets, beginning with Adam and including Jesus and Muhammad. The Bab was to be the founder of a new religion, Babism, which would conquer the world. But someday, declared the Bab, another great prophet would arise. Less than 20 years after the Bab's death, Husayn Ali declared himself to be that prophet chosen by God, the promised one of all the prophets. He took the name *Baha'u'llah,* which means "glory of God."

Baha'u'llah died in 1892 in Akko, Palestine, where he had been exiled. His son Abdul Baha came to America in the early 1900s to spread the religion. Since the death of Abdul Baha's grandson, Shoghi Effendi, in 1957, the Baha'is are no longer governed by a descendant of Baha'u'llah, but by an elected body of representatives from around the globe. Baha'is make pilgrimages to the tomb of Baha'u'llah in Akko and to those of the Bab and Abdul Baha on Mount Carmel in nearby Haifa. Presently there are several hundred thousand Baha'is in North America and more than five million in two hundred countries worldwide. Baha'i life centers around local counsels, which are called "spiritual assemblies."

In many respects, the Baha'i faith today is far removed from its Muslim origins. Unlike Islam, which is an exclusive faith, Baha'ism is ecumenical and attempts to unite all religions. As with Islam, according to Baha'i beliefs, there is only one God. Yet for the Baha'is, all religions share a common foundation and all the prophets of God proclaim the same faith. Humankind is one; people of all races, nations, economic groups, and religious backgrounds are equal in the sight of God.

To get to the "common foundation" of all religions, the Baha'is must deny or ignore fundamental differences among the world's religions. For example, some of the religious leaders whom Baha'is consider manifestations of the divine held contrasting views of God: Zoroaster proclaimed two supreme beings; Buddha held that God is not relevant; and Jesus and the Bible teach a personal, triune God. Baha'ism denies the miracles of Jesus Christ, his work of atonement on the cross, his physical resurrection, his glorious return, the resurrection of the body, the existence of the devil and of hell. In effect, it denies almost every biblical teaching.

The Sikhs

Although not strictly an offshoot of Islam, the Sikh religion has Muslim connections; moreover, it is not uncommon for Westerners to confuse the turbaned Sikhs with Muslims. The Sikh religion developed from the encounter of Islam with Hinduism and is a blending of the two.

Guru Nanak (1469–1539), the founder of Sikhism, was born in a village in Punjab, a region where northwest India borders Pakistan. At the time of his birth, the Indian rulers had become addicted to luxury and cared little for governing. Taking advantage of their weakness, Babur, the first of the Muslim Mughal dynasty, came from the north and captured much of northern India.

Guru Nanak saw this foreign domination as a judgment on the Hindu rulers, but he also rejected the fanaticism and intolerance of the conquering Muslims. In developing his ideas about God, he incorporated elements from both faiths. For example, he visited Mecca, yet taught that God's house is everywhere and not only in the direction of the Ka'abah. Similarly, he repudiated what he considered the meaningless rituals among the Hindus.

From this blending of two traditions came a new one, emphasizing one God (like Islam) but also the role of the guru, or teacher (like Hinduism). Like Hinduism, his religion teaches the transmigration of souls (reincarnation), but it rejects the Hindu abstinence from eating meat. Like Islam, Sikhism teaches submission to God and the reverence for the scriptures, yet the Sikh scriptures are ascribed to many teachers, not just one as is the case with the Qur'an.

Nanak was followed by nine other gurus, all of whom were instrumental in helping to develop the religion. After the tenth guru, religious authority passed to the Sikh community and its scriptures. What Sikhism has done is give a sense of identity to the people of the Punjab region, even when they have moved to other lands. Sikhs are known for their military prowess and their Golden Temple, built by the fifth guru, which stands as a symbol of their faith.

Worldwide Expansion

Today Islam is far and away the dominant religion of the Middle East and North Africa (see map). A sampling of some countries gives an idea of that dominance. In North Africa, for example, Algeria is 99 percent Sunni Muslim, with the other 1 percent Christian and Jewish; Tunisia is 98 percent Sunni Muslim, with 1 percent Christian and 1 percent Jewish. (These and other figures from 2001 are from Lunde, *Islam*.) Egypt's population is 94 percent Sunni Muslim with 6 percent Coptic Christian and others. The Coptic church is the ancient Christian church of Egypt, which recalls the days when the land, like much of North Africa, was Christian.

In Asia, Turkey is 99 percent Sunni Muslim and 1 percent other; this is the land where Paul brought the gospel on his missionary journeys. Saudi Arabia is 85 percent Sunni Muslim and 15 percent Shia Muslim. Other ancient lands of Christianity still maintain notable numbers of Christians. Jordan is 92 percent Sunni Muslim, 8 percent Christian and others. Syria is 74 percent Sunni Muslim, 16 percent other Muslim, and 10 percent Christian. Lebanon is 70 percent Muslim and 30 percent Christian.

Along with the little country of Bahrain, two well-known Middle Eastern countries are predominantly Shia Muslim.

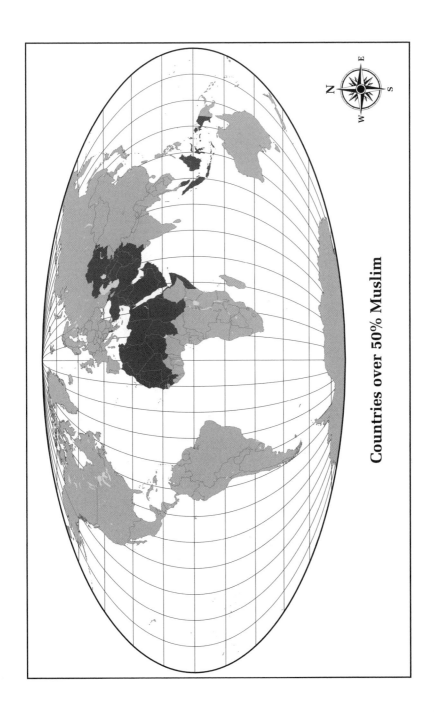

Countries over 50% Muslim

They are Iran (95 percent Shia, 4 percent Sunni, 1 percent other) and Iraq (66 percent Shia, 33 percent Sunni, 1 percent other), which border each other. Iraq is ancient Mesopotamia, the land of the Tigris and Euphrates Rivers, the birthplace of Abraham, and the land of famed Babylon and Nineveh.

As much as it is associated with the Middle East, Islam has larger numbers outside that part of the world. It may come as a surprise for many that the single country with the most Muslims is not in the Middle East. Rather, Indonesia is the country with the largest number of Muslims; 87 percent of its population—more than 184 million people—is Sunni Muslim. Even in the predominantly Hindu country of India, there are over one hundred million Muslims. In a few words, Islam is a worldwide faith.

This is evident in Islam's spread to Europe and America. Islam is the second largest religion in Europe, and the Muslim word in England is, "If we can take London for Islam, we can take the world" (Shorrosh 185). Meanwhile, Islam is challenging Judaism as the second largest faith in the United States. One Muslim leader speaks of how Muslims are committed to "founding a truly Islamic civilization" in North America (Gudel 6). Far from being a marginal presence as they were in the past, within the last few years Muslims have held Friday prayers inside the US Capitol building, and they delivered benedictions at the 2000 opening sessions of both the Democratic and Republican conventions.

Both in America and throughout the world, Islam is the fastest growing religion. Much of that growth comes through high birth rates among Muslims. In Europe and the United States, immigration and high birth rates combine for growing numbers. Joseph Gudel notes that while conversion has not been the main factor in that growth, there are "two major exceptions." The first is among African Americans and the second is among women who marry Muslim men and convert (8).

As of 2000, there were approximately 1.25 billion Muslims, 20 percent of the world's population. This compares with some 2 billion Christians (33 percent). These two religions, then, comprise over half of the entire population of the world.

While oil has brought a great deal of wealth to Muslim nations, it has also created problems. One is the dependency on Western technology. With that know-how comes the fear of becoming influenced by Western ideals and losing Muslim values. Following the fall of the Ottoman Empire, Turkey came under the leadership of Mustapha Kemal, better known as Ataturk (1881–1938), who believed that the only way for the country to progress was to Westernize it. His program included demanding the use of the Latin alphabet instead of Arabic, banning the Sufi orders, and forbidding women to wear the chaddar, the full-length woman's cloak with veil. Today the struggle between tradition and modernism continues in Turkey.

In Iran, Reza Shah introduced modernization, including the closing of Islamic schools and the forbidding of Islamic dress. He even forbade the pilgrimage to Mecca, which is, as chapter 6 will show, one of the pillars of Islam. His son Muhammad Reza Shah continued the program of modernization, which led to the 1979 revolution under Ayatollah Khomeini.

Much of the reaction to modernization has come in the form of a Muslim fundamentalist backlash. Known as Islamism, the rejection of secular governments has become a powerful force in Islam and the world beyond. Drawing their inspiration from the likes of Muhammad b. Abd al-Wahhab, Islamists reject any authority outside the Qur'an and the Sunna.

Clearly, Islam is a mosaic of many movements and varying beliefs. Nevertheless, Muslims hold in common a reverence for Muhammad, devotion to Allah, and belief in the Qur'an. Subsequent chapters will examine the basic teachings and practices of Islam and how they relate to the Bible.

Part 2.
Muslim Beliefs and Practices

4. The Qur'an

At the heart of the Christian faith is the Bible, God's revelation, which in the Old Testament prophesies the coming of the Messiah and then in the New Testament relates how those prophecies were fulfilled by Jesus Christ, the Savior of the world. At the heart of the Muslim faith is the book known as the Qur'an (sometimes spelled Koran, or Kuran). The Arabic word *Qur'an* means "reading" or "reciting," a reference to the command to read or recite said to have been given to Muhammad by the angel Gabriel.

Jews, Christians, Muslims: People of the Book				
Religion	**Scripture**	**Time**	**Language**	**Major Figure**
Judaism	Old Testament	1400–400 B.C.	Hebrew	Moses
Christianity	New Testament	A.D. 50–100	Greek	Jesus
Islam	Qur'an	A.D. 610–632	Arabic	Muhammad

Christianity recognizes the Old Testament as inspired Scripture foretelling the Messiah, the Christ, whose coming is reported in the New Testament. Judaism does not accept Jesus as the promised Savior and so rejects the New Testament. In theory, Islam accepts the Bible, but in practice it rejects the messianic nature of the Old Testament and its fulfillment in Jesus.

The Final Revelation

Unlike the Bible, which consists of 66 books written by several dozen inspired writers over the span of 15 centuries—from 1400 B.C. to A.D. 100—the Qur'an is the product of one man, Muhammad, written between the years 610 and 632. Moreover, while the Bible is arranged chronologically and by subject matter, the Qur'an follows no such arrangement. Rather, it is simply a collection of chapters, called *suras,* which in turn are divided into verses, called *ayat.* Muhammad declared that the various parts of the Qur'an were revealed over the course of time: "And it is a Qur'an that We [Allah] have divided, that thou mayest recite it unto mankind at intervals, and We have revealed it by (successive) revelation" (Sura 17:106).

Of the Qur'an's 114 suras, 86 were composed during Muhammad's time in Mecca and 28 in Medina. All but one of the suras (Sura 9) begins with the phrase *Bismillah . . .* which means "In the name of Allah, the Beneficent, the Merciful." Each sura has a title that is taken from a phrase within the chapter. For example, one of the best known chapters is Sura 96, known as "The Clot"; it tells of Muhammad's call: "Read: In the name of thy Lord who created; created man from a clot." Muslims refer to the suras not by their numbers but by their titles. Since most chapters are not coherent stories or unified messages, these titles generally do not designate the theme of the entire sura.

For the most part, the chapters are arranged according to length, with the longest toward the beginning of the Qur'an. The first 20 suras cover about as many pages as the remaining 94. Generally, the shorter suras come from the earlier Meccan period and the longer ones from the later time in Medina, which means that in reading through the Qur'an, one goes backwards in time. The Qur'an is approximately 85 percent the length of the New Testament or about one-third the length of the entire Bible.

Only in the Arabic language is the Qur'an considered God's word. All translations are referred to as interpretations, since they do not capture the perfect beauty of the original words of Muhammad, which translator A. J. Arberry describes as "the arresting, the hypnotic power of the Muslim scriptures" (*The Koran Interpreted* 2:8). Shorrosh describes the language of the Qur'an as "a kind of rhyming Arabic prose, the jingling sound of which greatly delights the Arabs" (*Islam Revealed* 25). According to the Qur'an, no human being, including Muhammad, could have created this sublime book: "and this Qur'an is not such as could ever be invented . . . Or say they: he [Muhammad] invented it? Say: then bring a surah like unto it, and call (for help) on all ye can besides Allah, if ye are truthful" (Sura 10:37-8).

Of course, eloquence does not mean truthfulness. And for all its beauty of expression, the Qur'an still makes for difficult reading; as one scholar puts it, "The Glorious Koran . . . is not easy to read. Especially in translation, where it inevitably lacks the compelling resonance and subtlety of the Arabic, it seems disjointed, repetitive, and stylistically inconsistent" (Lippman 56). Attractiveness of language aside, whether in Arabic or translation, the Qur'an contains the unique doctrine of abrogation, by which Muhammad was able to override or nullify earlier revelations with new ones: "Such of Our revelations as We abrogate or cause to be forgotten, we bring (in place) one better or the like thereof. Knowest thou not that Allah is able to do all things?" (Sura 2:106). This means that some of the Qur'an's injunctions still apply while others do not.

In spite of these difficulties, Muslims look to the Qur'an almost as Christians look to Christ (John 1:1)—God's eternal Word that has come to earth. They believe the Qur'an is an exact replica of God's heavenly book, which existed before the creation of the world and which rests on a "guarded tablet" (Sura 85:22). John Alden Williams summarizes the Muslim view as follows: "The central point of Islam from which all flows, the point of departure, may be paraphrased as follows: the God of Abraham . . . has spoken to man in the Qur'an. This divine Word is seen as the culmination of a long series of divine communications which began when God created humankind" (*Word of Islam* 7). Muslims consider the Qur'an God's final and most important revelation to humankind.

The sura that was placed first in the Qur'an is known as "The Opening of the Scripture" or "The Essence of the Qur'an" and has been called the "Lord's Prayer" of the Qur'an. Since it is recited at every important Muslim function, this sura has the additional label of "Seven [Verses] of the Oft-repeated." It captures much of the feeling of Islam and the Qur'an:

> In the name of Allah, the Beneficent, the
> Merciful.

58

1. Praise be to Allah, Lord of the Worlds,
2. The Beneficent, the Merciful.
3. Owner of the Day of Judgment,
4. Thee (alone) we worship; Thee (alone) we ask for help.
5. Show us the straight path,
6. The path of those whom Thou hast favoured;
7. Not (the path) of those who earn Thine anger nor of those who go astray.

Biblical Characters in the Qur'an

One does not have to read far into the Qur'an to see that it is a book of instruction, many regulations, words of praise to Allah, and admonitions about divine judgment. An example of both praise and instruction is Sura 112, "The Sincerity": "Say: He is Allah, the One! . . . He begetteth not nor was begotten. And there is none comparable unto Him." Already in this early Meccan sura, Muhammad was taking a stand against the Christian teaching of the Trinity, in which Jesus, the eternal Son of God, is begotten of the Father. Typical of the Qur'an's numerous descriptions of the judgment is another early Meccan sura, "The Traducer" (the slanderer): "Woe unto every slandering traducer. . . . He thinketh that his wealth will render him immortal. Nay, but verily he will be flung to the Consuming One. Ah, what will convey unto thee what the Consuming One is! (It is) the fire of Allah, kindled, which leapeth up over the hearts (of men)" (Sura 104:1-7).

It would be difficult to fill so large a book as the Qur'an with such succinctly stated dogmas and warnings. Not surprisingly, the Qur'an contains extensive narrative material consisting of stories or accounts. Very little of this material is drawn from Arabic sources; except for two stories of some length, there is nothing more than some brief Arabic allusions (Smith 56). The bulk, some 75 percent, of the Qur'an's subject matter comes from Jewish and Christian sources.

Muhammad saw himself as standing in the tradition of the Bible: "And argue not with the People of the Scripture unless it be in (a way) that is better, save with such of them as do wrong; and say: We believe in that which hath been revealed unto you; our God and your God is One, and unto Him we surrender" (Sura 29:46). Since the Qur'an is viewed as taking up where the Bible left off, it includes many incidents from the Bible as well as references to numerous biblical characters. These events and people are not presented in a chronological order as they are in the Bible. Rather, they are scattered throughout the Qur'an's 114 chapters.

Among the biblical characters who are mentioned or whose stories are told in the Qur'an are (Arabic names in parentheses) Adam; Abraham *(Ibrahim);* the angels Gabriel *(Jibril)* and Michael *(Mikail);* Amran *(Imran),* the father of Moses, Aaron, and Miriam; David *(Dawood);* Ezra *(Uzair);* Goliath *(Jalut);* Haman; Isaac *(Ishaq);* Ishmael *(Ismail);* Jacob *(Yaquob);* Jesus *(Isa);* Job *(Ayyub);* John the Baptist *(Yahya);* Jonah *(Yunus);* Lot *(Lut);* Joseph *(Yusef),* the son of Jacob; Mary *(Maryam),* the mother of Jesus; Moses *(Musa);* Noah *(Nuh);* Pharaoh *(firon)* the king of Egypt; Satan *(Iblis);* and Solomon *(Sulaiman).* Following are samplings of Qur'anic passages that pertain to some of those people.

Abraham *(Ibrahim)* is seen not only as the father of the Jews, but of the Arabs as well. The Qur'an often speaks of him; for example, Allah commands Muhammad, "And mention in the Book Abraham; surely he was righteous, a prophet" (Sura 19:41). Muslims consider Abraham neither a Jew nor a Christian but a *hanif,* that is, a true monotheist, who worshiped one God while living in pagan times. According to the Qur'an, God commanded Abraham to sacrifice his son Ishmael (Ismail), not Isaac as in the Bible, but spared him at the last moment (Sura 37:102-7).

Elsewhere, God is depicted as telling Muhammad to recite a list of other righteous men like Abraham: "Say (O

Muslims): We believe in Allah and that which is revealed
unto us and that which was revealed unto Abraham, and
Ishmael, and Isaac, and Jacob, and the tribes, and that which
Moses and Jesus received, and that which the prophets
received from their Lord. We make no distinction between any
of them, and unto Him we have surrendered" (Sura 2:136). No
distinction is made between someone like Abraham or Moses
or Jesus; they are all among the prophets.

Moses *(Musa)* is frequently mentioned in the Qur'an. He is
depicted as the prophet who was sent to lead the Israelites.
The Qur'an portrays Moses appearing before the Egyptian
pharaoh and performing miracles, including the dividing of
the sea. Allah says to the Israelites:

> O Children of Israel! Remember My favour where-
> with I favored you and how I preferred you to (all)
> creatures. . . . And (remember) when We did deliver
> you from Pharaoh's folk . . . And when We brought
> you through the sea and rescued you, and drowned
> the folk of Pharaoh in your sight. And when We did
> appoint for Moses forty nights (of solitude), and
> when ye chose the calf, when he had gone from
> you, and were wrongdoers. Then, even after that,
> We pardoned you in order that ye give thanks. And
> when We gave unto Moses the Scripture and the
> Criterion [discernment] (of right and wrong), that
> ye might be led aright. (Sura 2:47-53)

In this passage, the Qur'an echoes the Bible's account but, as
will soon become evident, often that is not the case.

Mary *(Maryam),* the mother of Jesus, has the honor of being
the only woman mentioned by name in the Qur'an. As a matter of fact, she is named more in the Qur'an than in the New
Testament! But there appears to be confusion between her and
Miriam, the sister of Moses and Aaron, who lived some 1,400
years before Mary the mother of Jesus. Since in Arabic both

names would be the same, and the New Testament Greek *Maria* is but a variation of the Old Testament Hebrew *Miryam*, it is not difficult to see how misunderstanding could arise, especially for someone who did not have the actual biblical texts available. Sura 66:12 speaks of "Mary, daughter of Imran," while the Bible mentions that Miriam was the daughter of Amran (Numbers 26:59). Sura 19, entitled "Mary," addresses her, "Oh sister of Aaron" (verse 28).

In an introductory paragraph to Sura 3, "The Family of Imran," translator Muhammad Marmaduke Pickthall discusses this discrepancy. He contends that the Qur'an uses the term "the family of Imran" as "a generic name for all the Hebrew prophets from Moses to John the Baptist and Jesus Christ." And he suggests that Jesus' mother did have a brother named Aaron. The charge of anachronism he dismisses as "absurd" (47). Whether or not one accepts the translator's explanations, such Qur'anic verses show the existence of a major theological problem for defenders of the Qur'an, namely, the many discrepancies between it and the Bible.

Contrary to the Bible, the Qur'an has Mary giving birth to Jesus under a desert palm tree (Sura 19:21-6; compare with Luke 2:1-7) and also depicts Mary as a person of the Trinity: "And when Allah saith: O Jesus, son of Mary! Didst thou say unto mankind: Take me and my mother for two gods beside Allah? he saith: Be glorified! It was not mine to utter that to which I had no right . . ." (Sura 5:116). Here Muhammad has Jesus denying that he and Mary are "two gods" in addition to Allah. Muslims view Christians as polytheists who worship three gods.

As for **Jesus** *(Isa),* "the Qur'an gives a greater number of honourable titles to Jesus than to any other figure of the past" (Parrinder 16). Among the many stories about Jesus, the Qur'an includes a non-biblical account of his childhood, which has Jesus saying, "Lo! I come unto you with a sign from your Lord. Lo! I fashion for you out of clay the likeness of a bird, and I breathe into it and it is a bird" (Sura 3:49).

For all it says about Jesus, the Qur'an denies what in the four gospels is central—the crucifixion of Jesus. "They slew him [Jesus] not nor crucified, but it appeared so unto them; and lo! those who disagree concerning it are in doubt thereof; they have no knowledge thereof save pursuit of a conjecture; they slew him not for certain. But Allah took him up unto Himself" (Sura 4:157-8). According to this passage, Jesus ascended into heaven ("Allah took him up") without ever dying. To Muhammad, Jesus was not the eternal Son of God or Savior of the world: "The Messiah, Jesus son of Mary, was only a messenger of Allah . . . say not 'Three'—Cease! (it is) better for you!—Allah is only One God. Far is it removed from His transcendent majesty that He should have a son" (Sura 4:171).

Even as it denies the crucifixion and the Trinity, in some ways the Qur'an ironically honors Jesus more than Muhammad himself. Although the Qur'an denies the crucifixion of Jesus, it accords him the honor of not having experienced the corruption of death. Nowhere does the Qur'an mention sin in connection with Jesus, but Muhammad is urged, "Ask forgiveness of thy sin" (Sura 40:55). Jesus is mentioned in the Qur'an 97 times, and Muhammad is mentioned 25 times. And while miracles are attributed to Jesus, beginning with his virgin birth (Sura 3:47), that is not the case for Muhammad.

Muhammad's Sources

Although some scholars such as Dr. Anis Shorrosh dispute the claim, Muhammad maintained he was illiterate, referring to himself as "the Prophet who can neither read nor write" (Sura 7:157). This was his way of underscoring the contention that, although he performed no miracles, the giving of the Qur'an through him, an unlearned man, was in and of itself the greatest miracle. While Muslims would say the book came directly from Allah through Gabriel to Muhammad, there are other ways to explain it.

Scholars have shown that some Qur'anic verses were taken from earlier Arabic poetry. W. St. Clair-Tisdall, an early 20th-century missionary to Persia, recounts a significant incident from the life of Muhammad:

> It is interesting also to note that some of the verses of the Koran have without doubt been taken from poems anterior to Muhammad's assumption of the prophetic office, in proof of which two passages in the *Sabaa Mu'allaqat* of Imra'ul Qays etc. are quoted, in which several passages of the Koran occur, such as, "The hour has come and shattered is the moon" ["The Moon," Sura 54:1]. It was the custom of the time for poets and orators to hang up their compositions upon the Ka'aba, and we know the seven *Mu'allaqat* were exposed. We are told that Fatima, the Prophet's daughter, was one day repeating as she went along the above verse. Just then she met the daughter of Imra'ul Qays, who cried out: "O that's what your father has taken from one of my father's poems, and calls it something that has come down to him out of heaven"; the story is commonly told amongst Arabs until now. (Warraq, *Origins of the Koran* 235-6)

Similarly, a number of contradictions between the Qur'an and the Bible can be accounted for when we consider some of Muhammad's contacts with other influences. Since the Bible was not yet translated into Arabic, the question naturally arises as to where Muhammad received his information about the Bible. During the years in Mecca, his revelations were still short, impassioned pleas, pronouncing Allah's judgment on those who did not accept monotheism. It was not until Muhammad moved to Medina that he began to develop the religion more fully. In doing so he had to come to grips with the Bible. If Muhammad was to stand in the line of the great monotheistic prophets of old, he had to know what they had said. Here Muhammad faced a dilemma. How could he build on the foundation of the "people of the book"—as he frequently referred to Jews and Christians—unless he knew what was in that book?

In working out his religion in Medina, the prophet had opportunity to interact with a considerable Jewish community, who had helped make the oasis town into "a leading agricultural centre" (Hitti 104). For a time, Muhammad even commanded that Muslims face Jerusalem while praying. But Jewish-Muslim relations were to prove less than friendly. "[The Jews] could not resist the temptation to show their superior cleverness by pointing out the factual inaccuracies in the Apostle's versions of the Old Testament stories" (Glubb 251). An example of Muhammad's Old Testament information not agreeing with the Bible is that the Qur'an has Noah as 950 years old at the time the flood began (Sura 29:14-5), while the Bible gives that number as the total length of his life (Genesis 9:29).

The information Muhammad did get from the Jews was not always from the Bible. Referring to extra-biblical Jewish writings, one historian notes, "Apparently the Jews who acquainted the prophet with the Bible also gave him snatches of the Talmud; a hundred passages in the Koran echo the Mishna and the Gemaras" (Durant 185).

Considering the hostility between the Jews and Muhammad, it would not be surprising if some had intentionally given Muhammad misleading information about the Bible. More likely is the possibility that the Jews of Arabia were not especially well-versed in the Old Testament. A later Jewish scholar referred to them as "ignorant," although still surpassing others of that region in religious knowledge (Geiger 4).

As for Christian contacts, through his own family Muhammad had some links with Christians (Abdul-Haqq 17ff). Khadija's hairdresser was a Christian. The first husband of one of Muhammad's later wives, Umm Habiba, had been a Christian. The same was true of his wife Sawda's first husband. The Prophet's last wife, Mary, was Coptic, that is, an Egyptian Christian. An adopted son, Zaid, came from a Christian family. Other relatives, such as Warqa ibn Naufal and Uthman ibn Al-Huwayrith, were also Christians. Christian apologist Abdul-Haqq describes still more contacts with Christians in Mecca:

> There was a considerable community of Christians living in [Muhammad's] own hometown so that they had a cemetery of their own. These Christians belonged to various denominations and were quite friendly with their neighbors. Once when the pagan Meccans were planning to rebuild the temple of Kaaba, they decided to entrust the project to a Coptic Christian whom they described as "a friendly craftsman." (15)

The actual size of the Christian "community" in Mecca is, of course, unknown. Likewise, the degree to which these Christians were knowledgeable about the Bible is also unknown. And one other unknown factor is how much Muhammad actually questioned them about their faith. Nevertheless, the Qur'an contains numerous references to the New Testament.

It is apparent that much of Muhammad's knowledge of Christianity came from heretical sources. St. Clair-Tisdall notes, "In the Prophet's day, numbers of Christians in Arabia were not only an ignorant people, but belonged to heretical sects, which, on account of their dangerous influence, had been expelled from the Roman Empire, and thus had taken refuge beyond the border land" (Warraq, *Origins of the Koran* 258).

It's quite possible that the heretical teaching of the Monophysites—that Jesus had only a divine nature and not a human nature—led to the misunderstanding that Mary, as the mother of God, was a member of the Trinity. The apocryphal infancy gospel of Thomas, written in the second century after Christ, relates the story of Jesus fashioning clay birds and turning them into living birds (Hone 60), and another apocryphal book tells of Jesus' birth beneath a palm tree. While neither Monophysite nor apocryphal influences can explain the greater discrepancy that Jesus was not crucified, another ancient heresy can. The second-century Egyptian theologian Basilides taught that Jesus exchanged roles with Simon of Cyrene before the crucifixion (Livingstone 168). One of the great tragedies of Islam is that Muhammad rejected biblical Christianity, whether from lack of knowledge of the Bible or from sheer hardness of heart.

The Compilation of the Qur'an

According to early sources such as Ibn Ishaq, Muhammad received his revelations under seven different conditions: in dreams; in visions; through an angel; through an angel "in the form of a young, tall man"; during his night journey and ascent into heaven; by Allah speaking from behind a veil; and through seizures (Caner and Caner 84). The last form, seizures, caused the prophet to sweat, hear bells in his ears, shiver, foam at the mouth, and roar "like a camel." Some have concluded that Muhammad suffered epileptic seizures. Moreover, Muhammad told his wife Khadija that he feared he might be possessed by demons (85).

During his lifetime, Muhammad's followers had taken to memory or had written down the various recitations of their leader. They wrote the prophet's "impassioned outbursts" on whatever materials were available—papyrus, palm leaves, stones, and even as tattoos on their chests (Hamdani). Other followers, known as "reciters," tried to memorize his recitations. Within a year or two after Muhammad's death, these recitations were collected, and during the caliphate of

Uthman, the Qur'an was compiled in its final form. The need for this was especially acute as a number of the reciters *(hafiz)* died in the Battle of Yamamah in 633. One of Muhammad's secretaries, Zayd ibn Thabit, was given the task of standardizing the Qur'an. According to Zayd, "During the lifetime of the prophet the Qur'an had all been written down, but it was not yet united in one place nor arranged in successive order" (Saleeb and Geisler 3:18); later, mainline Islam would adopt the view that even the order had been established in Muhammad's lifetime (chapter 8).

Many details concerning the compilation of the Qur'an remain unknown; *The Encyclopedia of Islam* states: "The history of the text and the recitation of the Qur'an after the death of Muhammad in 632 is still far from clear" (404). What is clear is that Muslim "classical literature records thousands of textual variants, which, however, are not found in any extant manuscripts known to Western scholars" (404). This is especially significant since Muslims maintain that the Qur'an as it exists today was never changed (a subject that will be treated in some detail in chapter 8). Nevertheless, most scholars, including non-Muslims, have accepted the main points of the traditional view, namely, that the Qur'an as it has come down to us is basically the same as the one Muhammad recited.

During the early years of Muslim conquests, the Qur'an was in its formative stages. Some of the first Muslims were more interested in their warfare than in their scriptures, as evidenced by the general Khalid b. al-Walid, who boasted of his ignorance of the Qur'an (Warraq, *Origins of the Koran* 73). Yet it was the Qur'an that would sustain the faithful through the centuries. Today millions of Muslims venerate the Qur'an. According to Shorrosh:

> The Qur'an is held in the greatest esteem and reverence among Muslims as their holy scripture. They dare not touch it without first being washed

and purified. . . . They read it with the greatest care and respect, never holding it below their waist. They swear by it and consult it on all occasions. They carry it with them to war, write sentences of it on their banners, suspend it from their necks as charm, and always place it on the highest shelf or place of honor in their homes. (quoted in Saleeb and Geisler 3:19)

Alfred Guillaume adds, "In many places children under ten years of age are required to learn by heart its 6,200 odd verses. . . . No event of consequence in family or public life passes without the reading of an appropriate passage" (74).

For all the worldwide reverence it receives, the Qur'an is at odds with the Bible, which is the center of Christian faith and life. Much of the remainder of our study will examine the differences between the two scriptures, trying to help us understand the Muslim mind and seek ways to convey to it the saving biblical truths.

5. Muslim Beliefs

Going back to Muhammad, the two basic doctrines of Christian faith that Muslims attack most sharply are the Trinity and the divinity of Jesus Christ. These doctrines are the core of Christian faith, and every non-Christian religion or philosophy seeks to overthrow them. In a debate with Christian Anis Shorrosh, Muslim Ahmed Deedat declared:

> In the Christian catechism of the churches they say, "The Father is God, the Son is God, and the Holy Ghost is God, but they are not three Gods, but one God. . . ." It continues, "the Father is a person, the Son is a person, and the Holy Ghost is a person, but they are not three persons, but one person." I am asking, What language is that? Is that English? It sounds English, but that is not English. Person—person—person, but not three persons, but one person. (Shorrosh 253)

One wonders what catechism he is referring to when he speaks of three persons being one person. Actually, the Athanasian Creed describes how "three persons are to be worshiped in one Godhead and one God is to be worshiped in three persons" (Tappert 20), not trying to explain but simply to state the mystery. Muslims never seem to tire of pointing to the unreasonableness of the Trinity, yet as St. Augustine said two centuries before the advent of Islam, "If you understand it, it's not God" (Anderson 37).

Islam seems to pride itself on being a simple religion, without the mysteries of the Christian faith. As will become apparent, however, simplicity is not always synonymous with truth. This chapter will examine the five basic beliefs of Islam and then look at the second source of Muslim teachings in addition to the Qur'an, the hadith.

The Qur'an states, "It is not righteousness that ye turn your faces to the East and the West; but righteous is he who believeth in Allah and the Last Day and the angels and the Scripture and the Prophets . . ." (Sura 2:177). A review of these five basic beliefs will help in understanding Muslims. In addition to the Pickthall translation of the Qur'an, this chapter will include several others, so that readers can get a brief taste of more translations.

The Five Basic Beliefs of Islam

1. Belief in Allah: one God
2. Belief in the Last Day: final judgment, heaven and hell
3. Belief in angels: Gabriel, Michael, Satan, the jinn
4. Belief in the scripture: the Bible and Qur'an
5. Belief in the prophets: Adam, Noah, Abraham, Moses, Jesus, Muhammad

---

Belief in Allah

For Muslims, Allah is the one true God. Along with Judaism and Christianity, Islam is considered one of the three great monotheistic religions. Because of this and their common Middle Eastern origins, it is frequently assumed that all three worship the same God. In fact, that is not the case, for the God of the Qur'an is not the God of the Bible.

Allah is seen as the almighty and all-knowing creator of all (the translation used in this section on Allah is from M. H. Shakir): "He created the heavens and the earth with truth, and He formed you, and made goodly your forms. . . . He knows what is in the heavens and the earth, and He knows what you hide and what you manifest; and Allah is Cognizant of what is in the hearts" (Sura 64:3,4). Allah is seen as the revealer of the Qur'an: " . . . Allah has revealed the Book with the Truth; and surely those who go against the Book are in a great opposition" (Sura 2:176). In the Qur'an, Allah speaks in different voices, sometimes in the first person singular (I), elsewhere in the first person plural (We), and at times in the third person (He). Muslims speak of the many "We" references as a majestic form of communication and not as any indication of a plurality within the Godhead.

Islam strongly condemns any doctrine of plurality within God and so completely rejects the Trinity. In uniting human nature with God, Christians are guilty of the greatest sin, *shirk,* that is, the cardinal sin of associating something with God in worship.

> O followers of the Book! do not exceed the limits in your religion, and do not speak (lies) against Allah, but (speak) the truth: the Messiah, Isa son of Marium is only an apostle of Allah and His Word which He communicated to Marium and a spirit from Him; believe therefore in Allah and His apostles, and say not, Three. Desist, it is better for you; Allah is only one God: far be it from His glory that He should have a son; whatever is in the heavens and whatever is in the earth is His; and Allah is sufficient for a Protector. (Sura 4:171)

> Certainly they disbelieve who say: Surely
> Allah, He is the Messiah, son of Marium; and the
> Messiah said: O children of Israel! Serve Allah,
> my Lord and your Lord. Surely whoever associ-
> ates (others) with Allah, then Allah has forbidden
> to him the garden, and his abode is the fire; and
> there shall be no helpers for the unjust.
> Certainly they disbelieve who say: Surely
> Allah is the third (person); and there is no god but
> the one God, and if they desist not from what they
> say, a painful chastisement shall befall those
> among them who disbelieve. (Sura 5:72,73)

In rejecting plurality within the Godhead, Islam has created a theological problem of its own. Contrary to the ruling
theology in Baghdad at the time, the noted Muslim scholar
Ahmad b. Hanbal (780–855), after whom one of the four
Sunni schools of law is named, held to the doctrine that the
Qur'an was uncreated, including its letters and sounds. He
was flogged and imprisoned for his belief, but when the inquisition (the *mihna*) came to an end, the popular "doctrine of
the uncreatedness was restored, and has not been challenged
since, in the Sunni world" (Glassé 268). Shiites, however,
continue to reject this teaching, because it is seen as a com-
promise to the idea that Allah is completely one. If there is an
eternal, uncreated word beside God, it would seem to come
close to what the Bible teaches when it says about Jesus, "In
the beginning was the Word, and the Word was with God, and
the Word was God" (John 1:1).

According to Muslim tradition, there are 99 names for God.
Known as the "best" or "most beautiful" names (Sura 7:180),
some of these names describe his essence and some his qual-
ities. Among other things, he is referred to as the Eternal (Sura
112:2), the Gracious (Sura 42:19), the King (Sura 59:23), the
Slayer (Sura 15:23), the First and the Last (Sura 57:3). (For a

complete listing, see Glassé 118-9.) Some of the titles are reminiscent of names that the Bible ascribes to God, but one biblical name for God is conspicuous by its absence: "God is love" (1 John 4:16).

An important attribute of Allah is his will. He is completely free to do as he pleases. The meaning of *Islam* is "submission to Allah's will." One of the most common expressions on the streets of Arab-speaking cities is *enshaalah*, "if Allah wills."

Although not forbidden in the Qur'an, Muslim tradition prohibits the use of images. Consequently, Muslims have developed the art of calligraphy to a high degree in decorating their mosques and many other places.

Belief in the Last Day

The Qur'an says much about the judgment and about heaven and hell. The Qur'an's poetic-prose seems to be at its most expressive when describing the day of judgment (except where indicated otherwise, the translation used in this section on the Last Day is from Williams, *The Word of Islam*):

> When the Trumpet is blown with a single blast,
> And the earth and mountains are lifted and
>   crushed with a single blow,
> On that Day shall befall what shall come to pass,
> And the sky shall be split, for on that day
>   it shall be frail . . .
> On that day you shall be exposed,
>   not one secret hidden. (Sura 69:13-18)

People will receive books recounting their good and bad deeds. Those whose books have more good will enter heaven:

> Then he who is given a book in his right hand
>   shall say, "Here read my book;

> Surely I believed and I would encounter
>   my reckoning."
> So shall they be in pleasant life
> In a sublime garden,
> Its clustered fruits nigh.
> "Now eat and drink with pleasure, for what
>   you did in days gone by." (Sura 69:19-24)

Among the many delights of paradise are the *houris,* the female companions of the saved: "They will recline (with ease) on Thrones (of dignity) arranged in ranks; and We shall join them to Companions, with beautiful, big and lustrous eyes" (Ali Sura 52:20). As for the unbelievers, their fate is expressed in the harshest terms:

> But he who is given his book in the left hand
>   shall say, "Would I was not given
>   my book,
> And never knew my account!
> Would death had been the end;
> My wealth avails me naught,
> My power is perished."
> Take him and fetter him,
> Then roast him in Hell!
> Then in chain of seventy cubits' length
>   insert him! (Sura 69:25-32)

According to this, unbelievers are chained to one another at intervals of about one hundred feet.

Both the Bible and the Qur'an teach the realities of judgment, heaven, and hell. But the similarities end there. The Qur'an does not agree with the biblical teaching that we are conceived and born in sin (Psalm 51:5). It also has a different concept of forgiveness. In Islam forgiveness is not God's undeserved gift through Jesus Christ, but it is something to be earned. Forgiveness is not a gift but a reward: "For such [the saved] the reward is forgiveness from their Lord, and gardens with rivers flowing underneath, an eternal dwelling: how excellent a recompense for those who work (and strive)!" (Ali Sura 3:136).

Belief in Angels

The angels of Islam, like those in the Bible, are spiritual, non-corporeal beings. They were created from light and serve and praise God, often as his messengers. The Arabic word for *angel* is *malak,* which is closely related to the Hebrew. Muslims believe that God revealed the Qur'an to Muhammad through the angel Gabriel (the translation used in this section on Angels is from Marmaduke Pickthall):

> Say (O Muhammad to mankind): Who is an enemy to Gabriel! For he it is who hath revealed (this Scripture) to thy heart by Allah's leave, confirming that which was (revealed) before it, and a guidance and glad tidings to believers; who is an enemy to Allah and His angels and His messengers, and Gabriel and Michael! Then, lo! Allah (Himself) is an enemy to the disbelievers. (Sura 2:97,98)

In mentioning Michael along with Gabriel, the Qur'an names the same two angels that the Bible names. Gabriel is depicted as a bearer of "glad tidings." In addition, the Qur'an names other angels not mentioned in the Bible.

That passage brings together two key biblical thoughts. The first has to do with glad tidings; Christians speak of the gospel as the "good news," for that is what the word means. The gospel (the *evangel*) is the glad tidings that we have a Savior. "Once you were alienated from God and were enemies in your minds because of your evil behavior," wrote the apostle Paul, "but now he has reconciled you by Christ's physical body through death to present you holy in his sight, without blemish and free from accusation. . . . This is the gospel that you heard" (Colossians 1:21-23). The other passage is a warning. "I am astonished," wrote Paul elsewhere, "that you are so quickly deserting the one [God] who called you by the grace of Christ and are turning to a different gospel—which is really no gospel at all. . . . But even if we or an angel from heaven should preach a gospel other than the one we preached to you, let him be eternally condemned!" (Galatians 1:6-8). In light of the biblical definition of the gospel and the warning against distorting it, Muhammad's claim of receiving his message from a heavenly angel is disturbing to say the least.

Like the Bible, the Qur'an speaks of the fallen angel, the devil, or Satan *(Iblis)*. In the Qur'anic account, however, Satan did not fall because of direct disobedience to God. According to the Qur'an, when God created the first man, the angels were commanded to bow down and worship the man. When asked to explain himself, Satan defended his refusal: "I am better than him. Thou createdst me of fire, whilst him Thou didst create of clay" (Sura 38:77). According to the Qur'an, Satan's fall was the failure to worship man.

Along with the angels, the Qur'an and Muslim tradition say much about the jinn, more invisible creatures, who, like Satan, were created from flames and who are able to assume various forms. Some of the jinn are evil and some good; the good ones go to heaven. Belief in the jinn was already widespread among the Arabs before the time of Muhammad. Much lore has come down about the jinn or, as we usually call them in English, the genies.

Belief in the Holy Books

Muslims believe in four holy books. These include the Qur'an and three portions of the Bible: the Pentateuch, or Law *(Tawrat)* of Moses, the Psalms *(Zabur)* of David, and the Gospel *(Injil)* of Jesus (the translation used in this section on Holy Books is from A. J. Arberry, *The Koran Interpreted*):

"O believers, believe in God and His Messenger and the Book He has sent down on His Messenger and the Book which He sent down before. Whoso disbelieves in God and His angels and His Books, and His Messengers, and the Last Day, has surely gone astray into far error" (Sura 4:135ff). Here Muhammad clearly refers to the previous books—namely, the Bible—and calls on people to believe.

As "people of the book," Jews and Christians are repeatedly called upon to pay attention to their scriptures: "But had the People of the Book believed and been godfearing, We would have acquitted them of their evil deeds, and admitted them to Gardens of Bliss. Had they performed the Torah and the gospel, and what was sent down to them from their Lord, they would have eaten both what was above them, and what was beneath their feet" (Sura 5:70ff). In other words, if the people of the book would have listened to the Scriptures, they would have been blessed.

At the same time, the Qur'an consistently contradicts the Bible. In spite of numerous allusions to the Bible, the Qur'an does not quote it directly; and although the Bible is considered a holy book, Muslims spend a great deal of time attacking it. This is in marked contrast to the way in which the New Testament treats the Old. The New Testament contains hundreds of references to and direct quotations from the Old; these allusions always convey a sense of deep reverence. In speaking of the Old Testament, Jesus declared, "The Scripture cannot be broken" (John 10:35); for Jesus and the early Christians, the Old Testament was reliable and authoritative.

Islam resolves this discrepancy by asserting that the present forms of the biblical books are corrupted *(tahrif),* either in the written manuscripts or in the interpretation (people today might call it "the spin") that Jews and Christians apply to them. Only the Qur'an is perfect, and where the previous revelations differ from it, *they* are in error.

The Muslim authority Abu Hanifa (ca. 752–840), founder of one of the four Sunni schools, summed up the high regard in which Muslims hold the Qur'an:

> The Qur'an is the word of God, and is His inspired word and revelation. It is a necessary attribute of God. It is not God, but still is inseparable from God. . . . It is written in a volume, it is read in a language, it is remembered in the heart, and its letters and its vowel points, and its writing are all created, for they are the works of men, but God's word is uncreated . . . its words, its writing, its letters, and its verses are for the necessities of man, for its meaning is arrived at by their use, but the word of God is fixed in the essence of God, and he who says that the word of God is created is an infidel. (quoted in Saleeb and Geisler 3:18-9)

If the Qur'an—the word that came through one man, Muhammad—is correct while the previous Scriptures are wrong, it is incumbent on Muslims to show how, when, why, and where the corruption took place. This is a subject we will return to in chapter 9.

Belief in Prophets

According to the Qur'an, Allah reveals his will to humankind through the prophets. Islam recognizes between 25 and 29 prophets, including some people that Christians might not think of as prophets (Miller, *Muslim Friends* 176-8). Many of these people are from the Bible: Adam, Noah, Abraham, Lot, Ishmael, Isaac, Jacob, Joseph, Moses, Aaron, David, Solomon, Job, Jonah, Elijah, Elisha, Zechariah, John the Baptist, Jesus. Concerning Jesus, the Qur'an states (the translation used in this section on Prophets is from Abdullah Yusef Ali): "Christ the son of Mary was no other than a

Messenger; many were the messengers that passed away before him" (Sura 5:75).

In addition to these biblical characters, there are other prophets, some whose identities are uncertain and others who may be identified with people from the Bible: Idris (possibly Enoch), Dhul Nun, Uzair (probably Ezra), Hud, Salih, Suf-Abib, Dhul Kift (possibly a son of Job), Dhul Qarnain, Luqman, and Muhammad. The name Uzair (Ezra) is of special interest; it is mentioned only once in the Qur'an: "The Jews call Uzair a son of Allah, and the Christians call Christ the Son of Allah. That is a saying from their mouth; (in this) they but imitate what the Unbelievers of old used to say. Allah's curse be on them: how they are deluded away from the Truth!" (Sura 9:30). Nothing in the Old Testament indicates that the Jews ever said that about Ezra. The verse also clearly illustrates that the Muslim god is not the God of Christians, since the New Testament frequently speaks of Jesus as the Son of God.

Of the prophets, five or six are considered the most important ones. They include Noah, Abraham, Moses, Jesus, and Muhammad; at times Adam is included in the list. The purpose of the prophets is to convey Allah's will to the people. Referring to Muhammad, the Qur'an says, "We did not send a Messenger but to be obeyed, in accordance with the will of Allah" (Sura 4:64). For Muslims, Muhammad is the final prophet. As the last prophet, he bears the title "the Seal of the Prophets." Since his prophecy, the Qur'an has brought an end to, or has sealed, all prophecy.

The Hadith

Second to the Qur'an as the source of Muslim belief and practice is the *hadith*. The Arabic word can mean "speech," "report," "narrative," or "tradition" (Netton 90). The hadith are the records of the sayings and deeds of the prophet and his companions. While all Muslims accept the authority of the

Qur'an, there is much dispute about the hadith. The controversy arises over which of the many thousands of hadith are authentic and which are not. According to Thomas Lippman:

> An elaborate set of standards was developed for examining purported sayings of the prophet and for sorting out the genuine from the spurious. In orthodox, or Sunni, Islam, six books of hadith are generally accepted, all compiled in the first three centuries after Muhammad's death. The two considered most trustworthy are those of al-Bukhari, who is said to have validated only seventy-five hundred sayings or traditions out of the half-million that he studied, and of Muslim ibn al-Hajjaj. (79)

The criterion used in determining the authenticity of the hadith is simple, at least in theory: Can the saying or event from Muhammad's time be traced back to someone who would have been a personal eyewitness? In addition, sayings that seemed to contradict the Qur'an were excluded, as were those coming from any person of questionable motives or morals. In practice, the selection process has not gone smoothly, and the entire subject of hadith is still the topic of heated debate among Muslims.

Each hadith consists of two main elements: the *isnad,* or chain of authorities, and the *matn,* the text itself, which may conclude with some moral. The following example shows all these elements:

> Bukhari, from Asbagh b. al-Faraj from Ibn Wahb from Yunus from Ibn Shihab from Abu Salama b. Abd al-Rahman from Abu Hurayra: a Bedouin came to the Messenger of God, may the benediction of God be upon him, and peace. He said, "Messenger of God, my wife gave birth to a dark-colored male-child, and I deny that it is mine!"

"Do you have camels?" the Prophet asked. "Yes."
"What color are they?" "Reddish." "Are they ever
ash-colored?" "Yes, that happens." "How do you
suppose that happens?" asked the Prophet.
"Messenger of God, something in the blood
changes them." "Then perhaps something in the
blood changed the boy," said the Prophet, and he
did not allow him to deny him. (Williams, *Word of
Islam* 56)

This hadith would be considered sound because it has a chain
of respected authorities *(isnad)* going back to the time of
Muhammad. The text *(matn)* is also supported by other
hadith. Because it is considered authoritative, its lesson or
moral would be applicable to other similar situations.

"Hadith," as Alfred Guillaume points out, "enshrines the
sunna or 'beaten track'—the custom and practice of the old
Muhammadan community" (*Traditions of Islam* 10); it serves
as a powerful conservative force in uniting present-day
Muslims from around the world with the practices of seventh-
century Arabia. Although Muhammad is not considered
divine, his every word or action is considered the Muslim's
guide. An example of a hadith that has become an integral
part of Muslim beliefs is the idea that there are 99 names of
God, as mentioned previously. What the prophet is reported
to have done or said assumes the aura of divine law that all
Muslims in succeeding generations should follow, such as
this axiom: "The Prophet said, 'Whoever would be glad to
have his livelihood expanded and his life prolonged should
maintain family ties'" (Cleary 15).

Interestingly, a number of hadith apply Christlike attributes to Muhammad. "Weary of hearing of the acts of love and
mercy, of supernatural power and forgiveness of Isa b.
Maryam, [some traditionalists] have made a Muhammad after
his likeness" (Guillaume, *Traditions of Islam* 135). Although

the prophet of Islam claimed no miracles, traditions arose that had him feeding many people with only a little bread, casting out demons, and miraculously supplying water in the desert. Other hadith ascribe Jesus' words to Muhammad. For instance, reminiscent of Matthew 18:21,22, one hadith says, "A man came to the prophet and said: 'O apostle of God, how often are we to forgive a servant?' He remained silent. Then the man repeated the question three times, and finally he answered, 'Forgive him seventy times every day'" (139). That the Bible is directly quoted more in the hadith than in the Qur'an itself evidences the growing influence and awareness of Christianity as Islam spread beyond Arabia.

The long line of transmitters and the numerous opportunities for forgery have opened the door for widespread misuse. For example, during the Abbasid dynasty, "an enormous number of traditions were forged to further Abbasid interests" and legitimize the empire, such as, "The prophet said to Abbas [from whose family the dynasty came]: 'In you shall rest prophecy and sovereignty'" (*Traditions of Islam* 10). Guillaume notes that "it is difficult to regard the hadith literature as a whole as a trustworthy and accurate record of the sayings and doings of Muhammad" (12). Some Muslims, like Rashad Khalifa, go so far as to call for the complete abandonment of hadith and for the return to the Qur'an as the only source of Islamic teaching *(Qur'an, Hadith, and Islam).*

Nevertheless, for many Muslims the hadith traditions have taken on an authority that challenges the Qur'an itself. Guillaume relates how "the everyday life of Muslims throughout the world is governed and directed by these traditions" (5).

In addition to the Qur'an and hadith, many Muslims look to two other sources of authority. One is *qiyas,* which means "analogy"; it is "the principle by which the laws of the Koran and Sunnah [drawn from the hadith] are applied to situations not explicitly covered by these two sources" (Glassé 372). The second is *ijma',* which means "consensus," usually understood as that of the legal scholars concerning a point of law; it can also mean the consensus of the community. Two doctrines that have been established by popular consensus are the sinlessness of the prophets and the veneration of saints, neither of which is found in the Qur'an or hadith (Glassé 209). Finally, when all other sources have been exhausted, there is *ra'y,* "human reasoning used as a source of law"; this comes down to the opinion of the individual Muslim jurist. Fundamentalist sects reject the use of these sources and insist that the Qur'an alone is the source of authority.

The Vast Gulf

In reviewing Muslim beliefs, it is clear that rather than complement the Bible, Islam contradicts it. In his characteristic forthright style, Luther summed it up:

> Mohammed highly exalts and praises himself and boasts that he has talked with God and the angels, and that since Christ's office is now complete, he has been commanded to bring the world to his faith, and if the world is not willing, to compel it or punish it with the sword; there is much glorification of the sword in it. Therefore the Turks think that their Mohammed is much higher and greater than Christ, for the office of Christ has come to an end and Mohammed's office is still in force.
>
> From this anyone can easily see that Mohammed is a destroyer of our Lord Christ and his kingdom, and if anyone denies the articles concerning Christ, that he is God's Son, that he died for us and still lives and reigns at the right hand of God, what has he left of Christ? Father, Son, Holy Ghost, baptism, the sacrament, gospel, faith, and all Christian doctrine and life are gone, and instead of Christ only Mohammed with his doctrine of works and

especially the sword is left. That is the chief doctrine of the Turkish faith in which all abominations, all errors, all devils are piled in one heap. (*On War Against the Turk* 176-7).

Even an introductory look at basic Muslim beliefs reveals the vast gulf between them and Christian doctrine. The next chapter will look at Muslim practices, which are the outgrowth of the faith.

6. Muslim Practices

Hadith literature covers a wide range of subjects—whether religious, social, or legal—dealing with everything from alms-giving to marriage to the final judgment. Among the most significant subjects drawn from the hadith are the five pillars of Islam, upon which Muslim life rests:

> Ubayd Allah ibn Musa related to us: Hanzala ibn Abi Sufyan reported to us on the authority of Ikrima ibn Khalid on the authority of Umar (May God be content with them both!):
>
> He said the Messenger of God (May Prayers and peace be upon him!) said, "Islam is built on five (things): the testimony (There is no god but God and that Muhammad is the messenger of God); the performance of prayer; giving alms; the pilgrimage; and the fast of Ramadan." (Lunde 33)

Since the Muslim way of life centers around these five basic religious practices, an examination of these pillars will help us in understanding Islam. Our review of the five pillars will include examples of application from the four great schools of Sunni law: Hanafi, Maliki, Shafii, and Hanbali.

Like the five basic beliefs, the five pillars *(arkan)* are not difficult to understand. They clearly show how Islam is a legalistic religion of works. This contrasts with Christianity, in which we are saved by trusting in Jesus and good works are but the outward evidence of a living faith. In addition to reviewing the five pillars, this chapter will consider two other much-discussed aspects of Muslim life: the place of jihad, "holy war," and the role of women.

The Five Pillars

1. The Creed *(Shahada)*: "There is no God but Allah, and Muhammad is his prophet."
2. Ritual Prayer *(Salat)*: five times daily—sunrise, noon, mid-afternoon, sunset, night
3. Almsgiving *(Zakat)*: $1/_{40}$ ($2^1/_2$ percent) to be given to the needy
4. Fasting *(Sawm)*: during month of Ramadan
5. Pilgrimage *(Hajj)*: once in a lifetime, if possible, trip to Mecca

---

The Creed *(Shahada)*

The Muslim word for *profession of faith* or *creed, shahada,* means "to bear witness or testify." When compared with the three creeds used throughout Christendom—the Apostles', Nicene, and Athanasian—the Muslim creed is simple: "There is no God but Allah, and Muhammad is his prophet." Each Muslim must say this at least once in his or her lifetime. In reality, devout Muslims say it many times each day.

The creed is a statement of belief. It is also a call to surrender: "The (true) believers are those only who believe in Allah and His messenger and doubt not, but strive with their wealth and their lives for the cause of Allah. Such are the sincere" (Sura 49:15).

Braswell points out that the imamate (the authority of Ali and his successors) is so important to Shiites that they add to the confession "a phrase that declares Ali the commander of true believers and the friend of God" (64).

Ritual Prayer *(Salat)*

The *salat* (or *salah*) includes not only prayer but the rituals that accompany it. Ritual prayer is distinguished from spontaneous prayer to Allah, which is called *dua.* Although prayer is often mentioned in the Qur'an, the duty to pray five times a day comes from the hadith. Prayers are to be given each day at sunrise, noon, mid-afternoon, sunset, and night.

These ritual prayers contain verses from the Qur'an, are recited in Arabic, are said facing Mecca, and may be offered from almost anywhere. Muslims may pray these ritual prayers individually or with other believers. In order to perform salat, a person must be in a state of ritual purity; this means having performed the cleansing or ablutions and being situated in a pure place. Bathhouses, cemeteries, and the like are places where salat is not permitted to be done.

The act of ablution, in and of itself, has many dos and don'ts connected with it. The following directive, which comes from the Hanbali school and dates back to the time of the Crusades, is but one small example: "It is not lawful to use vessels of gold or silver for purification or any other thing, following the word of the Prophet, God bless him and give him peace" (Williams, *Word of Islam* 70).

As for the prayers themselves, there are numerous conditions and directives, including (from the same Hanbali text):

> The consecrating act in prayer is to say *Allahu akbar* [God is greater]! No other expression is permissible. You should raise your hands as high as

© CORBIS

Muslim Men at Prayer

your shoulders or less, and then recite from the Qur'an. If you are in the morning-prayer, recite the opening *sura* of the Qur'an. . . .

Then recite a sura from the last part of the Qur'an [where the shortest *suras* occur]. . . . Recite it in an audible voice.

When this sura is finished, repeat "God is greater!" while leaning forward to begin the inclination *[ruku]*. . . . Be sure to preserve sincere humility in both the inclination and the prostration which follows. Do not pray while making the inclination . . . (Williams, *Word of Islam* 72-3)

The rites and directives cover every detail, every movement. The recitation of prayers from the Qur'an in Arabic is essential, since Arabic is considered "at once a sacred and a liturgical language" and the worshiper thus experiences "a *reintegration* into the uncreated" (Glassé 401).

Should the salat be interrupted, it needs to be repeated from the beginning. Talking to others, yawning, breaking wind, or laughing are all considered interruptions (Glassé 400). This may seem humorous, but it brings to mind the inattentiveness that many Christians have toward prayers (as in church). Muslim directives do emphasize that motivation is important, yet the complex rituals are also reminders of the highly legalistic system that Islam is.

Once a week, on Friday, Muslims gather to worship in the mosque. Whether simple or elaborate, mosques have the same basic features. Outside in the courtyard is an ablution fountain for ceremonial washing. The *minarets,* originally modeled after Christian church steeples, are the spires from which the call to prayer is made. For centuries this was the duty of the *muezzin,* whose voice would carry over the bustle of city sounds, but now loudspeakers often do the work. Inside the mosque is the prayer hall, the floor of which is covered with carpets or mats so that worshipers can comfortably perform the necessary prostrations. In the wall facing Mecca there is an ornate niche, known as the *mihrab;* it is readily visible so that worshipers know which direction to face.

To the right of the mihrab is a pulpit, called the *minbar,* from which the imam or leader delivers the Friday sermon. Although in theory Islam has no clergy, in practice the men who are learned in Muslim doctrine and practice guide the *umma,* the Muslim community, in its worship and life.

Almsgiving *(Zakat)*

The word *zakat* means "purification." The act of giving is said to purify what one retains. Muslims are required to give $^1/_{40}$ ($2^1/_2$ percent) of their possessions to wherever possessions are most needed, such as to the poor, debtors, or slaves. The following sample of regulations pertaining to zakat is from the Shafii school of law:

> Whoever has the obligation to pay zakat and is
> able must pay it; if not, they commit a fault for
> which they must answer. If anyone refuses to pay
> it and denies its obligatory character they have
> committed apostasy and may be put to death. If
> they refuse it from motives of avarice, they shall
> have the amount taken from them and be given a
> sentence at the judge's discretion. (Williams, *Word
> of Islam* 81-2)

In some Muslim countries, the zakat is a required tax. This tax
applies only to Muslims; other taxes are required of non-
Muslims living under Islamic rule.

Fasting *(Sawm)*

The Qur'an commands: "O ye who believe! Fasting is pre-
scribed for you. . . . The month of Ramadan in which was
revealed the Qur'an, a guidance for mankind . . ." (Sura 2:183-
5). During the lunar month of Ramadan, the ninth month in
the Islamic year, Muslims abstain from food, drink, music,
entertainment, and sexual relations from sunrise until sunset.
This is considered a method of self-purification.

The Muslims use a lunar calendar, and so Ramadan rotates
through the various seasons, at times occurring during hot
months and at times in the winter. (The Muslim lunar calendar
has three extra years for each century of the solar calendar.)
Pregnant and nursing women, those whose health is bad, and
others with special circumstances are exempt from the fast.
The Qur'an is divided into 30 sections of about equal length so
that Muslims can read it daily during Ramadan.

In addition to fasting during the month of Ramadan, there
are other voluntary fasting days. Muslims may fast as a way of
doing penance. At all times, Muslims are to refrain entirely
from pork and wine. It is said that they can enjoy wine in paradise if they deny themselves of it in this world.

The month of Ramadan ends with the *Id al-Fitr,* the second most important Muslim festival. This festival generally lasts for three days.

Pilgrimage *(Hajj)*

If physically and financially able, each Muslim is required to make a pilgrimage to Mecca during his or her lifetime: "Pilgrimage to the House [place where Abraham prayed] is a duty unto Allah for mankind, for him who can find a way thither" (Sura 3:97). Every year during the 12th month, *Dhu al Hijjah,* about two million Muslims from around the globe make the hajj, which consists of a series of complex rituals over a period of ten days. The hajj must be performed during this month or it only qualifies as a lesser pilgrimage.

The pilgrimage includes walking around the Ka'abah, a practice that goes back to pre-Islamic times. According to Muslim tradition, Adam originally built the structure, and later Abraham and Ishmael rebuilt it. The stone cubicle now stands within the confines of the great mosque in Mecca and is covered with a black cloth. The grave of Ishmael is next to the Ka'abah. During the pilgrimage, each person wears a white robe in order to avoid all social or racial distinctions. Non-Muslims are not allowed to visit the holy sites upon penalty of death.

The following directive is from a ninth-century (or in Islamic terms, third century A.H., After the Hijra) scholar of the Maliki school in North Africa:

> Malik says that on entering Mecca one should enter the Inviolate Mosque. . . . Then one touches the Black Stone at the corner of the Ka'ba with one's lips, if one is able; if not, one puts one's hand on it and touches it to his lips, without kissing it. One then circumambulates the Holy House keeping it on one's left, seven times. Three times

> are quick and four are walking. One touches the
> corner of the Ka'ba each time one passes it, in the
> way we have described, and says "God is greater!"
> (Williams, *Word of Islam* 86)

Numerous other rituals are involved. One is to run or walk quickly seven times between two hills near the Ka'abah. This symbolizes the frantic search of Hagar and her son Ishmael for water when, according to Islam, they were in the desert there. A few yards from the Ka'abah, pilgrims drink from the well of Zamzam, where water is said to have sprung up to satisfy the thirst of Hagar and Ishmael.

Pilgrims also travel 12 miles from Mecca to the plain of Arafat, where Adam and Eve were said to have come together after being driven out of Eden. At this spot Muhammad delivered his last sermon. The act of standing on this plain is supposed to bring to mind waiting for the day of judgment.

Another activity involves throwing stones at three stone pillars. These pillars symbolize the places where Satan tempted Ishmael to resist his father's will to sacrifice him. As the pilgrim throws each stone, he or she says *Allah Akbar,* "God is great." This represents resisting temptation.

The last day of the hajj marks the most important Muslim festival, *Id al-Adha,* which is celebrated by Muslims everywhere. An animal is sacrificed in commemoration of Abraham's offering of a ram after he had been willing to sacrifice his own son Ishmael (Genesis 22:1-19 says it was Isaac). The feast includes visiting and the exchange of gifts.

Once a person has made the hajj, he or she bears the title *hajji.* For many Muslims this is the major event in their lives, and they return home with stories to tell and gifts to share. Since only about two million Muslims make the pilgrimage each year, it is clear that most are never able to fulfill this rite.

Before the advent of planes and buses, pilgrims might have taken two years to make the hajj from distant lands. Some pilgrims also visit the city of Medina, where Muhammad; Fatima; and Abu Bakr and Umar, the first and second caliphs, are buried. For some Shiites, visiting the tombs of Ali and Husain in Iraq is of equal or more importance than making the pilgrimage to Mecca.

Muhammad declared the area around the Ka'abah as *haram,* that is, "sacred or forbidden." Based on a passage from the Qur'an, non-Muslims are not allowed in the holy cities: "O ye who believe! The idolators only are unclean. So let them not come near the Inviolable Place of Worship . . ." (Sura 9:28). According to historian Philip Hitti, "The injunction as interpreted is still effective. No more than 15 Christian-born Europeans have thus far [1930s] succeeded in seeing the two Holy Cities and escaping with their lives" (118).

Jihad: The Sixth Pillar?

Jihad is the belief that one should engage in a holy struggle to preserve Islam against non-Muslim beliefs. While orthodox Muslims consider jihad a literal, even military, struggle against unbelievers, some more liberal scholars interpret it as a spiritual struggle. The wording of the Qur'an, the life of Muhammad, and Islam's history favor an emphasis on the literal understanding.

Some Muslims believe that jihad is the sixth pillar of their faith. Indeed, one hadith describes it second only to belief in God: "Allah's Apostle was asked: 'What is the best deed?' He replied, 'To believe in Allah and His Apostle (Muhammad).' The questioner then asked, 'What is the next (in goodness)?' He replied, 'To participate in Jihad (religious fighting) in Allah's Cause' (Hadith of al-Bukhari 1.25)" (quoted in Saleeb and Geisler 4:29). By way of contrast, when Jesus was asked what the greatest commandment is, he replied: "'Love the Lord your God with all your heart and with all your soul and with all your mind.' This is the first and greatest commandment. And the second is like it: 'Love your neighbor as yourself.' All the Law and the Prophets hang on these two commandments" (Matthew 22:37-40).

In discussing jihad, Saleeb and Geisler note:

> Both in principle and practice Islam has used terrifying tactics to further its religious cause. Allah said in the Qur'an, 'I will cast a dread into the hearts of infidels. Strike off their heads then, and strike off from them every finger tip' (Sura 8:12). Indeed, such cruel and unusual punishment was commanded even against thieves: "As for the thief, both male and female, cut off their hands. It is the reward of their own deeds, exemplary punishment from Allah" (Sura 5:38). (4:29)

The Qur'an contains many passages that deal with the subject of jihad.

As Muhammad's power increased, his position on warfare became more open and aggressive (Bailey). At first, as leader of a minority in Mecca, he advocated no retaliation but urged mutual acceptance: "Say: O disbelievers! . . . Unto you your religion, and unto me my religion" (Sura 109:1-6). After moving to Medina, he permitted defensive fighting: "Sanction is given unto those who fight because they have been wronged; and Allah is indeed Able to give them victory" (Sura 22:39). Next, he commanded defensive fighting: "Fight in the way of Allah against those who fight against you, but begin not hostilities. Lo! Allah loveth not aggressors" (Sura 2:190).

The final directives are dated from after Muhammad returned to Mecca in 630 and cleansed the Ka'abah of its idols:

> By this time it was evident that the Jews would not accept Muhammad's claim to be a prophet, so the list of enemies now included all unbelievers—Jews and Christians as well as pagans. Now it is

no longer just defensive fighting but aggressive Jihad against all unbelievers [that] is commanded. Since this is the final teaching of the Qur'an regarding Jihad, it is still in force today. (Bailey 15)

The Qur'an states, "O ye who believe! Take not the Jews and Christians for friends. They are friends to one another" (Sura 5:51). And another late sura declares, "Fight against those who have been given the Scripture as believe not in Allah nor the Last Day, and forbid not which Allah hath forbidden by His messenger, and follow not the religion of truth, until they pay the tribute readily" (Sura 9:29).

In response to the Muslim argument that jihad is done in self-defense, Saleeb and Geisler ask, "What were Muslim forces doing sweeping across North Africa and Europe all the way to France where Charles Martel stopped them at the Battle of Tours in A.D. 732? This was scarcely a defensive action by any acceptable meaning of the term" (4:29). Yet from the initial years of conquest, Muslims have looked upon such warfare as commanded by God. For instance, Umar, the second caliph, viewed his conquests as jihad (Bat Ye'or 165).

Since Muslims cannot be sure if their good deeds sufficiently outweigh their bad, jihad is the only way they can be certain of heaven. The Qur'an says:

> Therefore, when ye meet the Unbelievers (in fight), smite at their necks. At length, when ye have thoroughly subdued them, bind a bond firmly (on them). . . . But those who are slain in the way of Allah—He will never let their deeds be lost. Soon He will guide them and improve their condition, and admit them to the Garden which He has announced for them [paradise]. (Ali Sura 47:4-6)

97

In a 1979 speech, Iran's Ayatollah Khomeini expressed confidence in the ultimate success of jihad in this world: "The governments of the world should know that Islam cannot be defeated. Islam will be victorious in all the countries of the world, and Islam and the teachings of the Koran will prevail all over the world" (Bat Ye'or 133).

The events of September 11, 2001, were an illustration of jihad being carried out. This Qur'anic warning to unbelievers must have been on the minds of the terrorists: "Wheresoever ye may be, death will overtake you, even though ye were in lofty towers" (Sura 4:78).

Islam and Women

When it comes to Muslim practices, one of the touchiest issues is that of the treatment of women. This is especially important since, as Guillaume notes, "The Qur'an has more to say on the position of women than on any other social question" (*Islam* 71). Muslim apologists speak of how Islam has elevated the position of women (Badawi, *The Status of Women in Islam*). That may well be the case when compared with pre-Islamic conditions in Arabia. Yet when we examine the issue in another light, there is much to be desired.

Muhammad himself did not set a good example. While married to Khadija, he remained monogamous. After that he had another 12 wives and several concubines. "For Muslims, monogamy is the ideal, polygamy the concession to human nature," asserts Pickthall in his introduction to Sura 66. ". . . Having set a great example of monogamic marriage, the Prophet was to set a great example of polygamic marriage." But this claim doesn't hold up. One wife, as noted in chapter 1, was the prophet's favorite, Aisha, who had been engaged to him since she was 6 and married him when she was 9 and he was 53. This is difficult to excuse, even with the argument that such marriages were common back then.

Another case of Muhammad's bad example is his marriage to Zaynab bint [daughter of] Jabsh. She had been the wife of Zayd, an adopted son of Muhammad. When Muhammad became infatuated with her, Zayd divorced his wife so that Muhammad could marry her. The prophet received a special revelation, in which Allah allowed this: "So when Zayd had performed the necessary formality (of divorce) from her, We gave her unto thee in marriage, so that henceforth there may be no sin for believers in respect of wives of their adopted sons. . . . There is no reproach for the prophet in that which Allah maketh his due" (Sura 33:37,38).

At the same time Muhammad was given the beautiful Zaynab, another special revelation allowed him to have more than the four wives that are allowed to other Muslim men: "a privilege for thee [Muhammad] only, and not for the (rest of) believers" (Sura 33:50). Perhaps this explains why, according to the hadith, Muhammad had the strength of 30 men in his relations with women (Braswell 74).

The affair with Zaynab touches on the issue of veiling, a practice going back to pre-Islamic times. When Muhammad unexpectedly met the unveiled Zaynab, the incident started. The Qur'an calls for modest apparel for women, but does not specify the extent or size of veils. That varies from one Muslim country to another.

Elsewhere, the Qur'an contains a passage on how husbands are to treat their wives:

> Men are in charge of women, because Allah hath made the one of them to excel the other, and because they spend of their property (for the support of women). So good women are the obedient, guarding in secret that which Allah hath guarded. As for those from whom ye fear rebellion, admonish them and banish them to beds apart, and scourge them. Then if they obey you, seek not a

way against them. Lo! Allah is ever High Exalted,
Great. (Sura 4:34)

Abdullah Yusuf Ali's translation tries to soften the passage by
adding a parenthetical note: "beat (lightly)." That is highly
unlikely, since the same Arabic word is used for the beating of
slaves and camels (Morey 29). According to the hadith,
Muhammad said that a man should "avoid disfiguring [a
woman] or beating her excessively or abandoning her except at
home" (quoted in Caner 138-9). Such behavior certainly differs
from the biblical injunction: "Husbands, love your wives, just
as Christ loved the church and gave himself up for her . . . each
one of you also must love his wife as he loves himself, and the
wife must respect her husband" (Ephesians 5:25,33).

As with every other part of Muslim life, there are many regulations relating to marriage and divorce. These regulations
are from the Hanafi school, the most widely adhered to of the
four schools:

> A man may not marry his slavegirl unless he
> sets her free first, and a woman may not marry
> her slave. . . .
>
> Marriage with a woman of the Book [Jew or
> Christian] is lawful, but not marriage with a
> Zoroastrian woman. . . .
>
> Similarly marriage with an idolatress is for-
> bidden, unless she accepts Islam or a religion of
> the Book. . . .
>
> A free man may marry four wives, free or slave,
> but no more. It is unlawful for a slave to marry
> more than two women. Malik holds that he may
> marry as many as a free man, even without his
> owner's consent. We, however, hold that slavery
> reduces both privileges and penalties by one half,
> so that the slave may marry two women and the
> free man four, to manifest the superiority of the

free state. The "marriage of enjoyment" [permitted
by the Shiites] is invalid. . . . (Williams, *Word of
Islam* 89-90)

This excerpt contains several interesting features. It illustrates
differences among the various Sunni schools and between the
Sunnis and the Shiites. The so-called "marriage of enjoyment" allowed by the Shiites is a temporary marriage that one
enters for a stipulated period of time. A businessman, for
instance, who is spending a month in a large city, such as
Teheran, can go to the mosque and arrange for a temporary
marriage of so-and-so-many days.

The selection also shows the difference in status between
men and women. Men have more freedom in whom they can
marry and how many spouses they can have. It should be
pointed out that men are not to marry multiple wives unless
they can afford it and only if they treat their wives fairly.

Men also have more control when it comes to divorce,
which involves the husband simply repeating the words "I
divorce you." While the formula is very simple, there are various types of divorce: laudable, acceptable, and irregular
(Williams, *Word of Islam* 91). One of the hadith forbids a man
to remarry his divorced wife until she has lived with another
man (Guillaume, *Traditions* 102).

Faith and Works

For the Christian, good works are a natural consequence of
having saving faith in Jesus. In responding to the "sinful"
woman who anointed Jesus' feet with perfume (Luke 7:36-50),
Christ tied faith and love together. To his host, who looked
down on the woman, thinking, "She is a sinner," Jesus said, "I
tell you, her many sins have been forgiven—for she loved
much." To the woman, Jesus said, "Your faith has saved you."
Saint Paul linked the two thoughts together when he wrote,
"For it is by grace you have been saved, through faith—and

this not from yourselves, it is the gift of God—not by works, so that no one can boast. For we are God's workmanship, created in Christ Jesus to do good works, which God prepared in advance for us to do" (Ephesians 2:8-10). And James bluntly stated, "Show me your faith without deeds, and I will show you my faith by what I do" (James 2:18). Faith in Christ produces a life of good works.

This life of good works begins with inward attitudes: "But the fruit of the Spirit is love, joy, peace, patience, kindness, goodness, faithfulness, gentleness and self-control" (Galatians 5:22). In outlining the life of good works, the New Testament does not present a list of laws for every circumstance. Instead, it presents principles. Rather than being told how to worship, we are simply told to gather for worship: "Let us not give up meeting together, as some are in the habit of doing, but let us encourage one another" (Hebrews 10:25). This leaves it up to individual congregations to determine whether or not they will worship on Sundays, in a traditional or contemporary service, with songs or sermons, etc. Rather than being told not to drink any wine at all, we have the principles of avoiding drunkenness and doing everything in moderation.

As this chapter has shown, Islam also speaks about faith and deeds. But the relationship between the two is entirely different. Faith is not a response to God's grace—his undeserved love for sinners, which he showed by giving his Son Jesus Christ as the sacrifice for our sins. Rather, faith or belief in Allah is a way of earning Allah's favor. It is simply another good work. Christian works flow from a thankful heart; Muslim works are done to curry Allah's favor. Muslim life centers around deeds. The Qur'an, hadith, and the numerous laws of Islam treat every aspect of life. Although there is talk of motives in Islam, the emphasis in the Muslim's life of works is external, beginning and ending with outward rituals.

Williams correctly notes: "The most characteristic activity of Christian scholarship has been theology; that of Islamic scholarship has been the Law" (66). In other words, the bulk of Christian study has been focused on theology, studying the nature of God and what he has done for man's salvation. Islam has focused on the place of the law, what we are to do in order to try to win God's favor. There is a definite appeal in the Muslim emphasis, for people by nature are inclined to the notion that we must somehow save ourselves. To that end, it is much more appealing to have a list of rules than a set of principles. Ultimately, however, such legalism fails to offer the assurance and confidence that even the smallest child can have in learning:

> Jesus loves me, this I know,
> For the Bible tells me so.

Part 3.
Muslims and Christians

7. Islam and Christianity

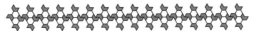

Many Christians living in America have little or no knowledge of Islam. Since the headline news of the war on terrorism, many Muslim terms and names, such as jihad, Shiites, Sunnis, and Ramadan have found their way into household conversation.

It may have come as a surprise to learn that the interchange between the two world faiths is not unique to this age.

Muhammad had some knowledge of Christianity, and the early Muslim conquests had a profound impact on Christianity. The ancient centers of Christendom—Jerusalem, Damascus, Antioch, Alexandria, Carthage—fell into Muslim control. In what had been the first strongholds of the Christian faith, the churches gradually died off.

What happened to the lands where Jesus and Paul had preached? Has Christianity been able to survive in Muslim-controlled lands? Has all the Muslim-Christian interaction been hostile? It is now time to examine the relationship between the two world religions. We will begin by examining their long and storied past before looking at the situation as it is today.

The Crusades

First Crusade (1095–1102): Capture of Jerusalem, Crusader state established

Second Crusade (1147–1240): Spurred by preaching of Bernard of Clairvaux; he was defeated

Third Crusade (1189–1192): Sultan Saladin recaptured Palestine; Richard the Lion-Hearted

Fourth Crusade (1202–1204): Crusade turned against Constantinople

Children's Crusade (1212): Ended in death or slavery for thousands of children

Fifth Crusade (1217–1229): Attacked Egypt, accomplished little

Sixth Crusade (1228–1239): Sultan granted Jerusalem, Bethlehem, Nazareth to Christians

Seventh Crusade (1249–1252): Led by Louis IX of France (St. Louis) against Egypt

Eighth Crusade (1270): Led by St. Louis, who died in North Africa

---

The Crusades

The first word that comes to the minds of many when thinking of Muslim-Christian interactions is *Crusades.* Seven centuries have passed, and yet their memory remains strong.

When taken in their context, the Crusades become more understandable. The 11th century was a time of upheaval in the Middle East. As opposing Muslim powers vied for supremacy, their struggles affected Christian sites. In the year 1009, the Church of the Holy Sepulcher in Jerusalem, which marked the burial place of Christ, was razed to the ground under a fanatical Egyptian caliph. Although rebuilding was allowed under new governorship, when the Seljuk Turks occupied the city in 1077, the city fell under a "harsh, unyielding, bigoted regime. Pilgrims returned to Europe with alarming tales of almost unbearable taxes and general oppression" (Maraini 100).

Meanwhile, in Europe, after long-standing differences came to a head, the pope in Rome and the patriarch of Constantinople severed ties in the Great Schism of 1054, marking the divide between Roman Catholicism and Eastern Orthodoxy that exists to this day. Within Europe there was constant conflict among Christian rulers.

When Constantinople was threatened by the Muslim Turks and appealed for help, Pope Urban II saw this as an opportunity to reunify Western and Eastern Christianity, with him as the head, as well as an opportunity to unify Europe's warring princes. In 1095, the pope convened the Council of Clermont, France, and there preached one of the most influential sermons of all time. He called for a crusade to win back Jerusalem from the Muslims:

> I say it to those who are present. I command that
> it be said to those who are absent. Christ com-
> mands it. All who go thither and lose their lives,
> be it on the road or on the sea, or in the fight

against the pagans, will be granted forgiveness for
their sins. This I grant to all who will march, by
virtue of the great gift which God has given me.
(Gonzalez 292)

The crowd responded with, *"Deus vult!"* God wills it! This
became the rallying cry for two centuries of Crusades.

The First Crusade did capture Jerusalem in what has been
described as a bloodbath, and a Christian kingdom was established in the Holy Land for about one hundred years.
Subsequent Crusades were less successful. The Muslim capture of the seaport of Acre in 1291 effectively marked the end
of the era of the Crusades. To this day, the ruins of Crusader
castles dot the route between Constantinople and Jerusalem
and stand as reminders of that bygone age.

For the Muslims, the Crusades did not have a huge impact,
since they did not affect a large part of the Islamic world.
Muslims were more absorbed in the confrontation between the
Fatimids of Egypt, a Shiite dynasty named after Muhammad's
daughter, and the Seljuk Turks. "In any study of the Arab
empires," notes Payne, "the Crusades have little place" (220).
While they may have "changed little" among the Muslim
empires, they did have a profound effect on Christian Europe.
They gave Europe a taste for the Orient and helped spur the age
of discovery in the search of a sea route to the East that would
bypass the Muslim lands.

For the most part, the legacy of the Crusades is negative.
For centuries they have tainted the Muslim view of Christianity. "Throughout the Middle East," notes Mark Albrecht,
"Christianity is known mainly for the Crusades." The Crusader sack of Constantinople in 1204 also deepened the divide
between Eastern and Western Christendom. Moreover, by
weakening the Byzantine Empire, the Crusaders paved the
way for the final Muslim conquest of Constantinople in 1453.
Urban's call for a crusade only served to blur the distinction

between church and state. Jesus had laid the foundation for that distinction when he said, "Give to Caesar what is Caesar's, and to God what is God's" (Matthew 22:21), and, "My kingdom is not of this world" (John 18:36). In Christianity, a spiritual leader has no call to be a warrior-prophet, nor is he in the business of declaring immediate entrance into heaven for dying in a holy war.

Indeed, Muslim apologists often respond to criticisms of jihad by pointing out that Christians did the same thing in the Crusades. In spite of the wrongness of the Crusades, there are several crucial differences between them and the Muslim concept of jihad. Saleeb and Geisler note four key distinctions:

> First of all, jihad is consistent with the teachings of the Qur'an. The Crusades, on the other hand, were not consistent with the teachings of Jesus. In fact, Jesus said to his disciples: "Put your sword back in its place for all who draw the sword will die by the sword" (Matthew 26:52).
>
> Second, jihad is consistent with the example of Muhammad himself, who practiced it in a literal way. But Crusades are contrary to the example of Christ who forbids retaliation (cf. Matthew 5:38-44).
>
> Third, jihad is a logical outworking of Islam while the Crusades are not biblical . . .
>
> Finally, Islam grew by its use of the sword against others. Christianity, by contrast, has grown most by the use of the sword against it. (4:30)

The same things that are said against the Crusades must be said about the Inquisition that grew out of them.

In connection with these subjects, at times the Old Testament wars of Joshua and the Israelites against the inhabitants of Canaan are brought up. As God had promised to Abraham four hundred years before that time, "Your descendants will come back here [to the Promised Land], for the sin of the Amorites [inhabiting the land] has not yet reached its full measure" (Genesis 15:16). Expelling the Canaanites from the land was God's judgment upon the people for their immorality, idolatry, and perversions, which included child sacrifice and religious prostitution. (For a listing of some of these evils, see Deuteronomy 18:9-13.) After four centuries during which the Canaanites did not change their ways, God used the Israelites as his instruments of judgment. This was a unique case and has not been repeated in history.

While speaking of the Crusades as "barbarous acts" that "cast shame upon the gospel of peace that Jesus brought," Shorrosh adds this final note to the topic:

> . . . the Crusades were not an all-out war against Islam. Originally, they were launched to force Muslims to let Christians visit and worship at sacred sites associated with Christ.
>
> The Muslims were wrong to deny or take advantage of Christians wanting to visit sacred sites. The Christians were also wrong to take up the sword against the Muslims who controlled these sites. It is wrong on both counts today.
>
> Today, to the credit of Israel, the sacred sites are open to all. . . . Only fear keeps Muslim, Christian, and Jewish worshipers back—fear of Islamic terrorists. (283-4)

The Dhimmis: Jews and Christians under Islam

Hand in hand with jihad comes the related topic of the treatment of people subjugated by the Muslims. *Dhimmi* refers to a member of one of the non-Muslim religions tolerated by the Muslim state in accordance with the *shari'a,* that is, the Qur'an and other Muslim sources of authority. The term *dhimmi* applies to Jews and Christians in Muslim lands. What has been and what is their status?

An oft-repeated idea about Islam is that the Muslims treat the Christians and Jews very well when these people live in Muslim lands. In discussing the Muslim conquest of Jerusalem under the caliph Umar in 638, one writer notes that, with certain qualifications, "The new masters of the city gave proof of much tolerance. . . . Christians and Jews ("People of the Book") were regarded quite differently than idolaters" (Maraini 99). Speaking of the Turkish invasion of Eastern Europe, Roman Catholic author Ovey Mohammed writes, "Whatever threat the Turks posed to Christians in Europe . . . the Ottoman Empire's policy toward People of the Book living within its borders was magnanimous. Balkan peasants used to say, 'Better the turban of the Turk than the tiara of the Pope' " (37).

"Better," however, is relative. Conditions of the dhimmi have varied from age to age and from country to country. Nevertheless, several general features have marked life under Muslim rule. In general, Jews and Christians have held the status of people of protected religions. One might ask, protected from what? The answer is, from their Muslim rulers.

That protection has come at a cost, namely, payment of certain taxes and an acceptance of an inferior social status:

> They ask thee (O Muhammad) of the spoils of war. Say: The spoils of war belong to Allah and the messenger, so keep your duty to Allah. . . . (Sura 9:1)
>
> Fight against such of those who have been given the Scripture as believe not in Allah nor the Last Day, and forbid not that which Allah hath forbidden by His messenger, and follow not the religion of truth until they pay the tribute readily, being brought low. (Sura 9:29)

When the Muslim armies made their march through the Middle East and beyond, the natives of the countries they conquered were given three options: convert to Islam, pay a heavy tax, or die. The poll tax *(jizya)* was, as the word implies, exacted according to numbers of people. A tenth-century Muslim jurist showed the close connection between jihad and jizya: "We Malikis [one of the four schools] maintain that it is preferable not to begin hostilities with the enemy before inviting the latter to embrace the religion of Allah except where the enemy attacks first. They have the alternative of either converting to Islam or paying the poll tax (jizya), short of which war will be declared against them" (Bat Ye'or 161). Because of the large revenue from this tax, at times Muslim governments may have discouraged conversion to Islam since it would have meant loss of income.

As non-Muslims under Muslim rule, dhimmis' land belonged to the state and they were not allowed to possess arms. Lacking any sense of real ownership or self-protection, the dhimmis found themselves "in a situation of permanent insecurity" (Bat Ye'or 52). Although free to practice their religion, that too had limitations: "Whatever Muslims rejected on religious grounds had to be hidden from public view and remain inconspicuous" (Busse 145). Depending on the place or circumstances, this might include no ringing of bells and no display of crosses.

Non-Muslims had to wear identifying clothing. Jewish and Christian men could not marry Muslim women, but Muslim men could marry Christian and Jewish women. Dhimmis could ride donkeys but not horses, and in some places had to stop, get off, and show respect to Muslims passing by. If he or she did not, the dhimmi was subject to beating (Bat Ye'or 212). At times, non-Muslims were subject to forced conversions and massacres in Islamic lands (267, 307, 330). Such treatment did not come about as a response to European colonialism or domination. Long before the rise of the European powers, Muslims had hatred for the dhimmis, whom they viewed as inferior. Often it was European colonization that freed the subjugated peoples.

While Christians and Jews could practice their religion, building new places of worship often was not allowed and existing places of worship fell into disrepair. Under Ottoman rule:

> No new churches could be built, and existing churches were liable to confiscation. Visible signs of the Christian faith were reduced to a minimum; no religious processions in the open air were permitted, and no ringing of bells. Christians were strictly forbidden to attempt to convert a Muslim, on penalty of death, but were themselves continually encouraged to apostatize. (McManners 155)

For a Muslim to convert has generally meant death for that Muslim as well. Under such circumstances, the all but total disappearance of Christianity from many Middle Eastern countries is understandable. This helps explain the stagnation of those churches that have survived in Muslim lands, where innovation and creativity are all but impossible. Commenting on the survival of the Greek Orthodox Church under Turkish rule, one historian notes, "Considering the worldly attractions of apostasy, the remarkable fact is not that so many fell away, but that so many continued faithful" (McManners 156).

Especially where Islamic fundamentalism has raised its head, there have been persecutions of Christians along with other non-Muslims. For instance, Coptic Christians have suffered in recent years in Egypt (Cofsky). The most horrifying example, however, is in Sudan, the largest country in Africa, where in recent decades Christians have been sold as slaves and some two million people have been put to death under the fundamentalist Muslim regime:

> Indeed, according to the 1999 report of the U.S. Committee for Refugees, a Washington-based advocacy group, the mostly Christian and animist

people of southern Sudan [the government based in the north of Sudan is the National Islamic Front] have suffered more war-related deaths during the last 15 years than any single population in the world—an estimated 1.9 million people having died there. Sudan's death toll is greater than the number of fatalities suffered in current and recent conflicts in Bosnia, Kosovo, Afghanistan, Chechnya, Somalia and Algeria combined. In addition, at least 4 million people now are internally displaced within the country, huddled in refugee camps because government armies and militias have driven them from their homelands—burning and looting their farms, slaughtering the men and kidnapping, raping and enslaving any women and children who did not escape. (Howd)

Because the Sudanese situation is so little known, it has been entitled the "hidden holocaust."

None of this is to say that Christians, Jews, or those of other faiths or philosophies have had a spotless record of fairness toward those who have different beliefs. History says otherwise. Moreover, Muslims I have known and been friends with have been generous, hospitable, and gracious. The point is that, contrary to the notion frequently set forth, life under Muslim rule has not been easy for non-Muslims. In his preface to Bat Ye'or's *The Dhimmi,* Jacques Ellul said it well, "The Muslim world has not evolved in its manner of considering the non-Muslim, which is a reminder of the fate in store for those who may one day be submerged within it" (33). Nor is it likely to "evolve." The Crusades were a step back from the Bible; Islam's treatment of non-Muslims is in keeping with the Qur'an.

Christians and Islam: Some Notable Examples

Through the centuries, there has been considerable interchange between Muslims and Christians. During the Middle Ages, many ancient Greek writings were translated into Arabic and eventually came to the West by way of Muslim scholars. The following cursory list identifies a few noted Christians who have related in various ways to the world of Islam.

John of Damascus (ca. 676–754) lived shortly after the Muslims had taken over the country of Syria and the illustrious city of Damascus. For a time he held the position of Christian representative at the court of the caliph. Encountering opposition because of his loyalty to his faith, John resigned and moved to a monastery outside Jerusalem. His many writings include hymns, such as "The Day of Resurrection," and a debate with Islam. His close contact with Muslims meant he "was able to understand Islam as it was experienced by his contemporary Muslims" (Sahas 129). Living under Muslim rule, he boldly debated Islam and called Muhammad a "false prophet" (79).

Francis of Assisi, founder of the Franciscan order of monks, lived during the Crusades. He believed that love, not war, was the way to deal with Muslims. After two unsuccessful attempts to evangelize Muslims, in 1219 he traveled to Egypt, where he was given an audience with the sultan. "Restricted by language barriers, Francis, nevertheless, made a feeble attempt at presenting the gospel. Though there is no evidence that any actual conversions resulted from his efforts, his example paved the way for others to view Muslims as potential brothers in Christ, among them *Raymond Lull,* an outstanding missionary of this period" (Tucker 53). Lull died a martyr; he was stoned to death in Algeria at age 80.

As the Crusades were winding down, the Dominican scholar *Riccoldo da Montecroce,* known as Brother Richard, wrote his *Refutation of the Qur'an (Confutatio Alkoran)* in 1300. His work shows a close and careful study of the Qur'an.

Brother Richard traveled in the Middle East, including Baghdad, and learned to speak and write Arabic. He was well qualified for his work. Depressed by what he saw in Islam, he wanted to "enable those misled by the Koran to more easily return to the true God" (x).

Martin Luther was involved in the monumental task of the Reformation. At the same time he took a studied interest in Islam. Some modern Christians have criticized Luther for the harsh manner in which he described Islam and the Qur'an— "an accursed and shameful book" (Mohammed 46), yet with his characteristic boldness, he called it as he saw it. He recognized that Islam is a complete rejection of the Christian faith: "In the article [teaching] that Christ is beneath Mohammed, and less than he, everything is destroyed. Who would not rather be dead than live under such a government, where he must say nothing about his Christ, and hear and see such blasphemy and abomination against him?" (*On War Against the Turk* 178).

Interestingly, like many other theologians before (including Brother Richard) and since, Luther viewed Islam as a form of heretical Christianity known as Arianism (Mohammed 30). Arius was a fourth-century presbyter in Alexandria, Egypt, who rejected the belief that Jesus is the eternal Son of God and taught that he was a created being. This heresy led to the Council of Nicea and subsequently, the Nicene Creed, which proclaims Jesus is "very God of very God, begotten not made" (Tappert 18). The similarity between Islam's and Arianism's view of Christ is readily apparent.

During his brief but brilliant life, the Anglican priest *Henry Martyn* (1781-1812) left England for India where he served as a missionary, established schools, and translated the New Testament into Hindustani, Persian, and Arabic. Having made the gospel available to millions of people, Martyn took ill and died while traveling overland through Turkey. Upon arriving in India, he had written in his journal,

"Now, let me burn out for God" (Tucker 134). Within six years that wish was granted.

Edward Granville Browne (1862-1927) was not a missionary but a scholar and adventurer. Nevertheless, he did much for Islamic studies. His book *A Year Amongst the Persians* is especially fascinating. It not only relates the social and religious lives of the Persians, but also offers a unique glimpse into the formative years of what would become a new world religion, Baha'ism. Browne personally met and spoke with the founder of the faith, Baha'u'llah.

Known as the "Apostle to Islam," the American *Samuel Zwemer* spent years doing missionary work during the late 19th and early 20th centuries. In spite of the loss of their two young daughters to disease within eight days of each other, he and his wife labored on. In Cairo, Egypt, he preached to crowds of over two thousand Muslims, proclaiming Christ while showing respect for the Muslims. Later he taught at Princeton Theological Seminary and, for over 40 years, edited the journal *The Muslim World*.

The late 19th to mid-20th centuries saw windows of opportunity for work in Muslim countries. Among noted missionaries to the Muslims was *Maude Cary,* whose work reached many in Morocco before the government closed its door to foreign missions in 1967. From 1919 to 1962, *William McElwee Miller* was a missionary to Persia (Iran). His work and books have been an inspiration to many.

The Situation Today

Recent years have witnessed the rise of Muslim fundamentalism, a movement characterized by the Muslims' desire to return to what they see as pristine Islam and by their distaste for what they consider impure. Expressing his opinion as a Shiite authority, the Ayatollah Khomeini (*Time* magazine Man of the Year in 1979) spoke of religious impurity: "Eleven things are unclean: urine, excrement, sperm, blood, a dog, a pig, bones, a non-Muslim man and woman, wine, beer, perspiration of the camel that eats filth" (Bat Ye'or 396).

Muslim countries are not known for their openness to Western influence. Espousing the fundamentalist Wahhabi brand of Islam, Saudi Arabia, the birthplace of Islam, is considered the most closed country in the world. No churches and no missionaries are allowed in the country. At the same time, Saudi Arabia spends millions of dollars of oil money promoting the building of mosques and the spread of Islam around the world (Braswell 2). According to a 2002 news release from the World Evangelical Alliance:

> Saudi Arabia is perpetually rated the most severe persecutor of Christians on earth. Religious liberty does not exist in principle or in practice. This not only leads to extreme persecution and suffering for believers, but also results in Saudi Arabia being one of the world's least evangelised nations, with over 21 million people and a growth rate 2.5 times the world average.
>
> Human rights and religious liberty groups regularly call for international pressure on Saudi Arabia to improve its appalling human rights. However, political and economic factors always seem to intrude because it is a strategic Western ally and the world's leading oil exporter . . .
>
> By law, a Saudi citizen must be a Muslim, and leaving Islam is apostasy, a capital offence. Sharia Law applies also to expatriate workers, whose religious expression is severely restricted. 'Proselytism' (witnessing) and public worship by non-Muslims is banned, although the Saudi Government does recognize their right to worship privately. However, the distinction between public and private worship is not clear, so that small

gatherings of believers for worship and fellowship in private homes are often raided by the Mutawwa (religious police), their materials confiscated and leaders detained. ("Saudi Arabia: New Year— Same Challenge")

Much of the focus of the Muslim-Jewish-Christian interchange today is Jerusalem, a special city to the three great monotheistic faiths. To Jews, it is the city of David and Solomon, the site of the ancient temples. To Christians, it is the place where the New Testament fulfillment of many Old Testament prophecies took place—where Jesus, the Messiah, or Christ, was crucified and rose again. To Muslims, Jerusalem is the place where Muhammad had his famous night journey and from which he is said to have been taken up into paradise.

Each faith has its own distinctive sites within the walls of the Old City, walls that date back to the time of the Turkish Sultan Suleyman the Magnificent. Jews from around the world flock to the remaining wall of the temple compound, the Western or Wailing Wall, as it is known, or simply The Wall, Hebrew *Hakotel.* For Christians, there is the Via Dolorosa, the Way of Sorrows, which leads up to the Church of the Holy Sepulcher. This church marks one of the two possible sites of the crucifixion and resurrection; the other site is the lesser known but more irenic Garden Tomb not far outside the walls. On the other side of the Wailing Wall, on Mount Moriah, stand the al-Aqsa Mosque and the oldest still-existing Muslim building, the Dome of the Rock, which commemorates the story of Muhammad's night journey.

The emotional attachment to such sites runs to the core of people's beings, and these holy places easily become sources of contention, as evidenced by the recent discovery of an ancient document from the temple of Solomon. The document, detailing repair plans for the building, dates from the time of King Joash of Judah (843–803 B.C.) and confirms the presence of the temple on Mount Moriah, long held by Jews and Christians to be the temple mount. Muslim authorities contend that the temple never stood there. According to a news release: "Muslim clerics have denied any Jewish historical connection to the site, revered by Jews as the location of their biblical temples" (BBC News).

Meanwhile, Islam continues to expand around the world. The first mosque in the United States was constructed in Cedar Rapids, Iowa, in 1934 (Hahn, *How to Respond to Muslims* 26). Since then, mosques have sprung up throughout the country, with New York and California having the largest numbers of Muslims. The growing Islamic presence in North America reminds North American Christians that Islam is no longer a religion "over there." Muslims are now our neighbors in the literal sense of the word.

The relationship between Muslims and Christians (as well as other non-Muslims) throughout the centuries has not been smooth. At best it has been uneasy and at times it has been violent and filled with terror. Given the huge rift between Islam and Christianity, the uneasiness is comprehensible. While some might think the solution is to ignore the differences, there is a better way. It is vital for Christians to understand the differences and then to share their faith, speaking the truth in love.

8. Islam Evaluated

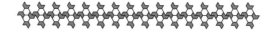

Throughout the course of this study, numerous conflicts with the Bible have been addressed. Islam sees itself as the fulfillment of Christianity, a religion that had the prophet Jesus but which was corrupted by people who call themselves Christians. Does Islam belong on this lofty pedestal? A final examination and evaluation of Islam will answer that question.

This chapter will focus on specific areas of difficulty for Islam, in particular, the problem of how a religion that claims to fulfill another can so consistently contradict it. The next chapter will examine whether or not the claims presented against the Bible and the Christian faith stand up. In both chapters, the discussion will include the somewhat technical subject of textual criticism. This is the study of the reliability of the texts of the Qur'an and of the Bible. Sooner or later, every comparison of these two religions comes around to this: How solid are the foundations of faith in Allah and of faith in Jesus Christ?

Muhammad and Jesus	
Muhammad	Jesus
Born in normal way	Miraculous virgin birth
Performed no miracles	Performed many miracles
Led followers into war many times	Did not fight
A sinner needing to repent	Without sin
Died and was buried	Died and was buried and rose again

The Possibilities

When comparing Islam and Christianity, there are four possibilities: (1) Both are right. (2) Both are wrong. (3) Islam is right, and Christianity is wrong. (4) Christianity is right, and Islam is wrong. Before making a concluding examination of Islam, a brief look at these options is in order.

> 1. *Both Islam and Christianity are right.* This is a popular view. Frequently we hear that both believe in and worship the same God. In fact, many people believe that all religions are basically the same and worship the same God—by whatever name(s) they use. The world's third largest religious group, Hinduism, would agree with this; since Hindus consider everything as a part of God (pantheism), ultimately everything is right. All is one. All paths lead to God, etc.

When it comes to the three great monotheistic faiths—Judaism, Christianity, Islam—there are a number of similarities that lead many to conclude that they all worship the same God. All three religions sprang up in Middle Eastern soil. All three are religions of revelation, each believing that God has revealed himself through written Scripture. All speak of many of the same personages, as Christianity refers back to the Old Testament and the Qur'an makes references to the Old and New Testaments.

Even Pope John Paul II in an address to young Muslims in Casablanca in 1985 said, "Your God and ours is the same, and we are brothers and sisters in the faith of Abraham" (Mohammed 61). Ovey Mohammed explains how such a statement is possible, given the Muslim rejection of the Trinity and deity of Christ: "Members of each community are children of Abraham according to their own self-understanding" (61). In other words, Christians are Abraham's offspring when, in Saint Paul's words, they "belong to Christ" (Galatians 3:29). And a Muslim is of the family of Abraham when he or she is a good Muslim—which means accepting an unbiblical account of Abraham and rejecting the person and work of Christ! Perhaps Joseph Smith and the Mormons are also included, since Smith "translated" the "Book of Abraham," an ancient Egyptian document that had nothing to do with Abraham (Cares 110).

Such doublespeak is appealing, but it only sweeps important differences under the carpet. The modern world has done so much of this that people are knocking their heads on the ceiling. In effect, Ovey Mohammed goes on to deny the Christian faith when he calls into question the truth and value of the incarnation and the Trinity and when he refers to "the fact that a growing number of Christians no longer accept that Christ is both human and divine. As for the doctrine of the Trinity, they find it virtually meaningless" (66). Even if this assertion were accurate, it would not prove his point. Polls of what people believe or don't believe do not determine truth.

Ultimately, saying that both are right is no different from saying that both are wrong. Instead of taking earnestly the claims of either religion, that way of thinking tries to create its own new reality—namely, that sincere belief in something somehow makes it true.

2. *Both Islam and Christianity are wrong.* This
   might be called a rationalist approach. Denying
   the very possibility of God revealing himself to
   humankind, rationalists assert that both the
   Qur'an and the Bible are the products of fallible human beings and are not to be considered
   God's word. Human advancement is not to be
   found in some revelation from beyond but in
   the application of reason. It is reason, not faith,
   that is to be our guide.

In his book *Why I Am Not a Muslim,* published by the secular humanist publisher Prometheus Press, Ibn Warraq offers
numerous forceful arguments against Muhammad, the
Qur'an, and Islam. But he also takes some space to attack the
historical reality of Jesus. This is the same approach that writers, such as the famous French skeptic Voltaire (1694–1778),
took during the Enlightenment.

Nevertheless, the idea of God and revelation are not easily
dismissed. The evidence that there is a God is powerful.
Nature attests that there must be a Creator, since the world
cannot create itself. The Bible says, "The heavens declare the
glory of God" (Psalm 19:1; Romans 1:18-20). And people's
consciences make them aware that they must answer to someone higher than themselves: "The requirements of the law [of
God] are written on their hearts, their consciences also bearing witness" (Romans 2:15). The arguments against God are
not convincing.

What people know about God from nature and their consciences is that he is powerful, wise, and just. But that is not
enough to show them how to find God and his love. Muslims
claim that the beautiful Arabic of the Qur'an is enough to
convince people that it is God's revelation to humankind. As
the next chapter will make clear, the Bible offers much more
than that to witness to its claim of being God's Word.

3. *Islam is right, and Christianity is wrong.* This is the Muslim position. In contending it has the final revelation from God, Islam asserts that the Jews and Christians have altered and twisted the previous revelations so that they contradict the Qur'an. That this is not the case will also become clear when we examine the Bible and its claims.

At any rate, Muslims assert that there has been no tampering with the Qur'an and that God has given the perfect book. The fact is, however, that whether the Bible is right or wrong, the Qur'an cannot be correct. To put it bluntly, there is *no way* that Islam can be correct.

In his hard-hitting book, *The Islamic Invasion,* Robert Morey gets to the heart of the issue. He calls it "a logical dilemma"; it is also a tragedy of almost incomprehensible proportions:

> The Muslim is trapped at this point. If he admits that the Bible originally said that Jesus died on the cross, then the Qur'an is in direct conflict with the older revelations.
>
> But Muhammad promised that this would not happen. Why? The Qur'an must agree with the older revelations because they all supposedly came from the same God.
>
> On the one hand, if the Muslim rejects the Bible, he must also reject the Qur'an because it appeals to the Bible as God's Word.
>
> On the other hand, if he accepts the Bible, he still must reject the Qur'an because it contradicts the Bible. Either way, the Qur'an loses. (135-6)

Muhammad himself was commanded: "And if thou [Muhammad] art in doubt concerning that which We reveal unto thee, then question those who read the Scripture [that was] before thee. Verily the Truth from thy Lord hath come unto thee. So be not thou of the waverers" (Sura 10:95). Elsewhere the Qur'an declares, "And unto thee [Muhammad] have We revealed the Scripture with the truth, confirming whatever Scripture was before it . . ." (Sura 5:48).

In spite of claiming to honor the Scriptures, Muslims will argue vehemently against the Bible. There is much at stake. The Christian who knows the Bible has nothing to fear from the Qur'an or Islam. Scripture promises, "The grass withers and the flowers fall, but the word of our God stands forever" (Isaiah 40:8). Jesus declares that "everyone who hears these words of mine and puts them into practice is like a wise man who built his house on the rock. The rain came down, the streams rose, and the winds blew and beat against that house; yet it did not fall, because it had its foundation on the rock" (Matthew 7:24,25).

> 4. *Christianity is right, and Islam is wrong.* This is the position that Bible-believing Christians hold. Contrary to Muslim allegations, the biblical text is reliable (chapter 9). Since the biblical text is earlier and is reliable, then the teachings of Muhammad, coming six centuries later, must be wrong.

In saying that the Bible is right and the Qur'an is wrong, there is no room for gloating, just as there is no room for compromising one's convictions for the sake of being nice. For Christians, the point is not to win an argument but to share the love of Christ.

Problems in the Qur'an

As noted in the chapter on the Qur'an, Muslims consider the book a "miracle." Most Muslims believe that it is eternal. Those who do not believe Muhammad's message are challenged to produce something better: "And if ye are in doubt concerning that which We reveal unto Our slave (Muhammad), then produce a surah of the like thereof, and call your witnesses beside Allah if ye are truthful. And if ye do it not—and ye can never do it—then guard yourselves against the fire prepared for disbelievers, whose fuel is of men and stones" (Sura 2:23). Such assertions are powerful, but they do not prove the point. The Qur'an has a number of serious flaws, a few of which will be discussed here.

The text of the Qur'an. Muslims assert that the text of the Qur'an is perfect and immutable. Even the order of the books, which is neither chronological nor thematic, is considered divinely planned. In *An Introduction to the Qur'an,* Abul a'la Mawdudi sets forth the standard Muslim view, namely that

> the surahs of the Qur'an were not arranged in the present order by his successors but by the Prophet (p. [peace be upon him]) himself under the guidance of Allah. . . . Thus it is an established fact that the surahs of the Qur'an were arranged in the present form on the same day that the Qur'an was completed by the one to whom it was revealed under the guidance of the One who revealed it. . . .
>
> It is, therefore, wrong to suppose that the surahs were arranged in the existing order after the death of the Prophet (p.) . . . the Prophet (p.) recited the whole Qur'an twice before Gabriel during the last Ramadán of his life. . . .
>
> Imam Malik says: "The Qur'an was compiled in the way the Companions heard it from the Prophet." (13-5)

According to Mawdudi, the only thing that varied among the first editions of the Qur'an was dialect of Arabic. Like ancient Hebrew, the basic written Arabic language is consonantal and vowels need to be added in order to avoid confusion. This is called "pointing"; for example, the letters TP in English could be read top, tap, or tip. Supposedly, the pointing was done in such a way as "the reading of the Qur'an (with a few minor variations) is the same as practised and taught by the Prophet (p.)" (17). In fact, that is not the case. Arthur Jeffery spent years collecting material and in *Materials for the History of the Text of the Qur'an* concluded:

> Very little examination is needed to reveal the fact that this [traditional] account is largely fictitious. Nothing is more certain than that when the Prophet died there was no collected, arranged, collated body of revelations. . . .
>
> The prophet had proclaimed his messages orally, and, except in the latter period of his ministry, whether they were recorded or not was often a matter of chance. . . .
>
> Now when it comes to the accounts of Uthman's [the third caliph] recension [version], it quickly becomes clear that his work was no mere matter of removing dialectical peculiarities, but was a necessary stroke of policy to establish a standard text for the whole empire. . . .
>
> There can be little doubt that the text canonized by Uthman was only one among several types of texts in existence at the time. (5-8)

What happened to the other versions? Uthman had them burned. If all the copies had been the same, except for minor variations in dialect, etc., why did he have them burned? It would have been better to keep them. "For should anyone have started up with the assertion, that Othman [sic] had altered the Koran," wrote 19th-century missionary C. C. Pfander, "it would have been possible, by bringing forward the old copy, to silence the accuser. But the fact that Othman caused all the former copies to be burnt, is proof that the new copies did not agree with them" (13).

Some alternate copies of the Qur'an, however, survived at least in part or are referred to in other Muslim writings, and it is these bits that have led Jeffery and others to their conclusions. Jeffery relates how, when he and another scholar came across a variant text in a library in Cairo, they were refused permission to photograph it and the manuscript was "withdrawn from access" (Morey 121). Among known variations, one sura is said to have originally had 200 verses but only 73 found their way into the Qur'an as it is now; and Shiites claim that Uthman left out about one-fourth of the original Qur'an "for political reasons" (121).

In 1972, workers in Yemen came across some ancient manuscripts of the Qur'an. Understandably, Muslim scholars have shown little interest in the find, and only two non-Muslims have spent considerable time with the documents. Not until 1997 were microfilm images of the manuscripts allowed to leave the country. James White writes, "This find also gives evidence of variation from today's Qur'an in both the reading of the text and its order, something unthinkable in traditional Islamic doctrine" (3:37).

In spite of variants in the Qur'an, the text that has come down to us is probably an accurate reflection of what the prophet said. But it is not, as Muslims claim, directly from Muhammad to us.

In addition to such variant texts, the problem of *revelations convenient to Muhammad* has already been noted. When Muhammad wished to take another wife, there was a convenient revelation. Not only was this the case with Zaynab, but it was also the case with his wife Mary, a Christian slave that had been given to him by the ruler of Egypt. Some of his other wives resented the attention that Muhammad gave to the beautiful Mary, who bore him a son that died in childhood, but a revelation brought an end to the complaining: "It may happen that his Lord, if he divorce you, will give him in your stead wives better than you, submissive (to Allah), believing, pious, penitent, inclined to fasting, widows and maids" (Sura 66).

The second problem relates to the doctrine of *abrogation,* by which some later revelations could annul earlier ones. We may recall Muhammad's position on warfare changing as he became militarily stronger—that is one example of his abrogation, but the most famous illustration of Muhammad's abrogation is the Satanic verses.

In 1989, Salman Rushdie's *The Satanic Verses* (dubbed as the most famous book most people will never read) caused a furor around the world. Its publication resulted in a *fatwa,* an opinion issued by a religious authority, in this case from the Ayatollah Khomeini:

> The author of The Satanic Verses, a text written, edited, and published against Islam, against the Prophet of Islam, and against the Koran, along with all the editors and publishers aware of its contents, are condemned to capital punishment. I call on all valiant Muslims wherever they may be in the world to execute this sentence without delay, so that no one henceforth will dare insult the sacred beliefs of the Muslims. (Dunn)

Much of the controversy centers on the book's title, which refers to a passage in the Qur'an. When many of Muhammad's followers fled to Abyssinia for their safety, the prophet wanted to do what he could to protect the Muslims. Under strong pressure, he compromised with his opponents in Mecca and acknowledged the existence of three pagan goddesses alongside Allah: "Have ye thought upon Al-Lat and Al-Uzza and Manat, the third, the other?" (Sura 53:19,20).

Later Muhammad regretted what he had said and confessed his error. He said he had been misled by Satan, and he abrogated the references to the three pagan goddesses:

Never sent We a messenger or a Prophet before thee but when He recited (the message) Satan proposed (opposition) in respect of that which he recited thereof. But Allah abolisheth that which Satan proposeth. Then Allah establisheth His revelations. Allah is Knower, Wise; that He may make that which the devil proposeth a temptation for those in whose heart is a disease, and whose hearts are hardened. . . . (Sura 22:52,53)

In effect, Muhammad was admitting that he could not always distinguish between the voice of Allah and that of Satan. Hence, the Satanic verses found their way into the Qur'an. What Rushdie's book did was dare to question the Qur'an. The question might be raised, how could Muhammad and his followers be sure that the entire Qur'an was not of Satan? When Luther and others have pointed to the Satanic origins of the Qur'an, they have merely been recognizing what Muhammad himself suggested.

Conflicts with the Bible

For all its reverence *for* the Bible and references *to* the Bible, the Qur'an strikes one for its lack of actual use *of* the Bible. Over a century ago, Henry Preserved Smith observed:

Although (as we have seen) a large part of this book [the Qur'an] is derived ultimately from the Bible, yet in no instance does it show, on the part of its author, such exact knowledge as would come from the study or even the reading, of its text. He [Muhammad] makes but one or two quotations from it. Even when he professes to give the substance of certain parts of it—as the covenant between God and Israel—he reproduces them very imperfectly. (168)

In discussing the Qur'an (chapter 4), a number of its discrepancies with the Bible came to light. There are many more, a few of which we will review.

Conflicts with Old Testament: According to Genesis chapter 1 and Exodus 20:11, God created the world in six days. The Qur'an agrees: "Lo! your Lord is Allah Who created the heavens and the earth in six days" (Sura 10:4). But elsewhere in the Qur'an, the days of creation add up to eight days: "Disbelieve ye verily in Him Who created the earth in two Days, and ascribe ye unto Him rivals? . . . He placed therein firm hills rising above it, and blessed it and measured therein its sustenance in four days. . . . Then He ordained them seven heavens in two Days" (Sura 41:9-12).

The story of Joseph is but another example of an account that has many points of contradiction between the Bible and the Qur'an. Here are a half dozen of the discrepancies from among those noted by Gleason Archer (506):

Bible (Genesis 37)	Qur'an (Joseph, Sura 12)
Joseph went to look for his brothers	The brothers persuaded their father and took Joseph with them
They plotted after Joseph arrived	They planned it beforehand
They put Joseph in a dry well	They put Joseph in a well with water
Joseph was sold for a considerable price	Joseph was sold for a little
Potiphar's wife tore the front of his cloak	She tore the back of the cloak (which proved his innocence)
Pharaoh told his dream to Joseph	The butler told the dream

Other Old Testament stories contain similar discrepancies. Archer contrasts a portion of the Qur'an's account of the Exodus from Egypt (Sura 26:55-60) with that of the biblical book of Exodus:

> In Egypt, the Israelites were stated by Pharaoh to be but "a scanty band" (in contrast to Ex 1:9). As they are permitted to leave Egypt, they are said to be forsaking "their gardens and splendid dwellings." Apparently, they had not been subjected to slavery at all (for no mention is made of it), but rather had enjoyed wealth and luxury in Egypt. (This renders the whole motive for deliverance of God's covenant people from Egypt rather obscure.) (507)

Among the many other contradictions are those that confuse time periods, such as referring to crucifixion during the time of Moses and Pharaoh (Sura 7:124)—a means of punishment used by the Romans more than 1,000 years later. Muhammad has Haman at the court of Pharaoh in Egypt at the time of Moses (Sura 29:39), while the Bible places him in the Persian court centuries later (the book of Esther). Moreover, the Qur'an seems to have Haman trying to build the Tower of Babel in Egypt: "And Pharaoh said: O Haman! Build for me a tower that haply I may reach the roads, the roads of the heavens" (Sura 40:36,37). The Bible places the Tower of Babel in Mesopotamia centuries earlier (Genesis 11).

Conflicts with New Testament: The Qur'an contains less New Testament material than Old, but what it does have shows the same types of confusion. For instance, the Qur'an has Zechariah unable to speak for three days (Sura 3:41); the Bible says that he was unable to speak until his son John the Baptist was born, which would be a period of about nine months (Luke 1:18-20).

The Qur'an has Jesus denying that he is the Son of God (Sura 5:19); in the Bible, when Jesus was asked during his trial, "Are you then the Son of God?" Jesus responded, "You are right in saying I am" (Luke 22:70). The Qur'an's most serious mistakes have to do with Christ's crucifixion and the Trinity, topics that have already been discussed.

In the face of such overwhelming evidence, the Qur'an claims to fulfill and supercede the Bible. The Qur'an was dictated by one man over the course of 22 years (610–632) to a people who did not have the Bible available in their own language. The dissimilarity is striking when one reads in the Bible how the people of Berea responded to the message of the apostle Paul and his missionary companion Silas:

> On arriving there, they [Paul and Silas] went to the Jewish synagogue. Now the Bereans were of more noble character than the Thessalonians, for they received the message with great eagerness and examined the Scriptures every day to see if what Paul said was true. Many of the Jews believed, as did also a number of prominent Greek women and many Greek men. (Acts 17:10-12)

The Bereans and others were able to compare the teachings of the early Christians with the Old Testament Scriptures. Today the opportunity is available to compare the New Testament with the Old Testament, and the Qur'an with the entire Bible.

Islam's Concept of Sin and Forgiveness

All but one of the Qur'an's suras begin in the name of Allah "the Beneficent, the Merciful." Yet it is one thing to speak of God's mercy and another to have a basis for that mercy. The Bible not only speaks of God's mercy and grace, but it embodies those attributes in the person of Jesus Christ.

The third chapter of the Bible speaks of the fall into sin (Genesis 3), and subsequent passages relate the fallen nature of the human race, for example: ". . . there is no one who does good. God looks down from heaven on the sons of men to see

134

if there are any who understand, any who seek God. Everyone has turned away, they have together become corrupt; there is no one who does good, not even one" (Psalm 53:1-3).

Having established the sinfulness of all people, the Old Testament foretold that the Messiah would come who would suffer and die for our sins. Written seven centuries before Christ came, Isaiah 52:13–53:12 sounds as if it were written after the fact as it describes the suffering and glorified servant of the Lord. Speaking of a future event, the prophet Isaiah enlists what is called the "prophetic perfect," using the past tense to show the certainty of God's promises:

> See, my servant will act wisely;
> he will be raised and lifted up and highly
>   exalted.
> Just as there were many who were appalled
>   at him—
> his appearance was so disfigured beyond that of
>   any man
> and his form marred beyond human
>   likeness— . . .
> But he was pierced for our transgressions,
> he was crushed for our iniquities;
> the punishment that brought us peace was
>   upon him,
> and by his wounds we are healed. . . .
> and the LORD has laid on him
>   the iniquity of us all. . . .
> For he was cut off from the land of the living;
> for the transgression of my people he was
>   stricken.
> He was assigned a grave with the wicked,
> and with the rich in his death,
> though he had done no violence,
> nor was any deceit in his mouth. . . .

after the suffering of his soul,
he will see the light of life and be satisfied.

Through his lowly death on the cross, Jesus offered his sinless
life, a sacrifice prefigured in the Old Testament sacrificial system. Nailed to the cross and crucified with criminals
(Matthew 27:32-44), buried in a rich man's tomb (Matthew
27:57-60), Jesus, then, arose from death (Matthew 28:1-10).

Islam denies the innate sinfulness of humankind. One
Muslim apologist writes: "The idea of original sin . . . has no
room in the teachings of Islam. Man according to the Qur'an
(30:30) and the prophet [Muhammad], is born in a natural
state of purity" (quoted in Bywater 3:10). It is not surprising,
then, that Islam completely rejects the substitutionary death
of Christ.

Instead of Christ, the Qur'an offers a system of salvation by
works. Judgment day is depicted as having scales on which
people's good and bad works will be weighed against one
another: "We shall set up scales of justice for the day of
Judgment, so that not a soul will be dealt with unjustly in the
least. And if there be (no more than) the weight of a mustard
seed, We will bring it (to account): and enough are We to take
account" (Ali Sura 21:47).

The Qur'an asserts, "Then those whose scales are heavy,
they are the successful. And those whose scales are light are
those who lose their souls, in hell abiding" (Sura 23:102,103).
It follows that if one has lived an evil life, there is no room for
a deathbed repentance or late-in-life turning. "In Islam sin is
not paid for, it is weighed on a balance scale" (Caner and
Caner 150).

Good works include believing in Muhammad's message
and doing what the Qur'an says. Pilgrimage is one such good
deed: "Lo! (the mountains) As-Safa and Al-Marwah [the two
hills near the Ka'abah] are among the indications of Allah. It
is therefore no sin for him who is on pilgrimage to the House

136

(of God) or visiteth it, to go around them (as the pagan custom is). And he who doeth good of his own accord (for him), lo! Allah is Responsive, Aware" (Sura 2:158).

While claiming to honor Jesus, the Muslim approach going back to the Qur'an in fact discredits him. In Jesus' words: "These people honor me with their lips, but their hearts are far from me" (Matthew 15:8, quoting Isaiah 29:13). What confidence can there be when at the close of their fixed prayers, Muslims are to include this prayer for their prophet: "O Lord, have mercy upon and give peace to Muhammad" (Saal 127)? No such prayer exists for Christ.

9. The Bible: God's Revelation

If the Qur'an and the entire Muslim faith are to stand, then the Bible must be discredited. For if the Bible is trustworthy in the form in which we have it, Islam must be wrong. Consequently, Muslims have developed an ambiguous approach to the Bible. On the one hand, they pay it lip service as being a previous revelation from God. On the other hand, they constantly look for errors in the biblical text in an effort to discredit it and show that it has been corrupted.

Any comparative study of the two religions at some point has to examine the biblical text. Books have been devoted to this subject, but the most we can do here is offer a cursory look at some of the basics. After considering the biblical text, this chapter will point out that the Bible does indeed teach the doctrines of the Trinity and the divinity of Jesus. This chapter will also discuss whether or not the Bible foretells the coming of Muhammad.

Some Prophecies of Jesus		
	Old Testament Prophecy	*New Testament Fulfillment*
Virgin birth:	Isaiah 7:14	Matthew 1:22,23
Christ as Prophet:	Deuteronomy 18:15-19	Acts 3:21-23
Birth in Bethlehem:	Micah 5:2	Matthew 2:1-6
Entry into Jerusalem:	Zechariah 9:9,10	Matthew 21:6-9
Betrayal:	Zechariah 11:12,13	Matthew 26:14,15
Christ's side pierced:	Zechariah 12:10	John 19:37
Christ's resurrection:	Psalm 16:10	Acts 2:27

The Doctrine of Corruption

From the time of Muhammad, one of the issues facing Muslim leaders has been the many discrepancies between the Qur'an and the Bible. Since God had given the former Scriptures as well as the Qur'an, the problem could not be attributed to God. Consequently, the notion developed that the Jews and Christians had corrupted their Scriptures. The Islamic doctrine of corruption is known by the Arabic term *tahrif,* which *A Popular Dictionary of Islam* defines as this:

> Corruption, distortion, alteration, especially as applied to the sacred texts. Muslims invoke the concept of tahrif to account, for example, for the disparity about Jesus in the New Testament and that in the Qur'an: Islam believes that Christians have altered the original text of a proto-Gospel (al-Injil) now lost. In v. 13 of Surat al-Ma'ida the Jews are also accused of textual corruption. (241)

140

The verse referred to says, "And because of their [the Jews] breaking their covenant, We have cursed them and made hard their hearts. They change words from their context and forget a part of that whereof they were admonished. Thou wilt not cease to discover treachery from all save a few of them. But bear with them and pardon them. Lo! Allah loveth the kindly" (Sura 5:13). The Qur'an does not directly accuse the Christians.

There are two approaches to tahrif (Abdul-Haqq 38). One approach maintains that the text itself of the Bible has been tampered with. The other approach is that, while the text is intact, Jews and Christians have twisted its meaning, making it say things that are not really there.

The idea of Christians changing the text of the Bible invites questions: When was it changed? Some contend that the changes took place before the time of Muhammad. But that only begs the question: Why was it changed? Since Muhammad had not yet appeared on the scene, the Christians and Jews would hardly know what to change so that it would disagree with Muhammad. As for changing it after Muhammad, that only presents more problems. Why, for instance, would Paul want to invent a crucified Christ when by his own admission this only made evangelism more difficult among Jews, who considered it "weakness," and Greeks, who thought it was "foolishness" (1 Corinthians 1:18-25)?

In arguing that the text has been altered, Muslims appeal to the so-called higher critical scholars, often members of liberal Christian denominations, who call into question the reliability of the biblical manuscripts. Since the 19th century, Muslims have used the arguments of such critics against Christianity:

> Muslim polemical [argumentative] works . . . always pursue this fundamental attitude: Christian theologians themselves admit that the Old and New Testament is not inspired as we have it today, but both parts of the Bible are full of errors, mis-

> conceptions, contradictions, and absurdities, if not
> willful distortions. Thus Muslim theologians see
> their interpretation of the Christian Scriptures con-
> firmed by Western scholarship. (Waardenburg 276)

These rationalist scholars would not limit their criticism to
the Bible "as we have it today." They would say it *never* was
inspired, for they reject the very notion of inspiration and
attempt to account for all religion not in terms of the divine
but in terms of human origins. What many Muslims have
failed to see is that given the opportunity, those same scholars
would apply their skepticism to the Qur'an as well. As a matter of fact, they are doing it already (Warraq). They are no
more likely to believe the doctrine of the virgin birth of Jesus
in the Qur'an than the version in the Bible. Moreover, the
attacks upon the Bible's integrity have themselves run into
dead ends. Even if such destructive scholarship were to prove
valid, that would not confirm the Qur'an. It would, as chapter
8 pointed out, merely undermine the Qur'an and Islam.

As for the accusation of tampering with the meaning, we
see an example of this approach in a Muslim-Christian debate.
In reference to Jesus' words in John 8:58—"before Abraham
was born, I am"—Muslim apologist Jamal Badawi spoke of the
"before" as a preeminence in greatness rather than in time,
even though the context clearly indicates that Jesus was
speaking about his being alive before Abraham, who had lived
some two thousand years earlier (Badawi and Brug). In such
cases, the Muslim apologist tries to prove that Christians have
twisted the original meaning in an attempt to bolster the doctrine of Christ's divinity.

In arguing against the crucifixion and resurrection of
Christ, H. M. Baagil enlists both types of tahrif, as seen in this
excerpt from *Christian Muslim Dialogue:*

> M [Muslim]. We all agree that nobody saw the
> moment he [Christ] was resurrected. They

found the sepulcher where Jesus was laid down, empty and made the conclusion that he was resurrected because the disciples and other witnesses saw him alive after the alleged crucifixion. Could it not be possible, as the Qur'an claims, that he didn't die on the cross?

C [Christian]. Where is the proof then?

M. Let us see passages in the Bible supporting this evidence. Do you give more weight to what Jesus said or to hearsay of the disciples, apostles and other witnesses?

C. Of course more to Jesus himself.

M. That is in accordance with what Jesus said (Matthew 10:24): "The disciple is not above his master, nor the servant above his lord."

C. But Jesus himself said that he will rise from the dead (Luke 24:46): "And said unto them, thus it is written, and thus it behoved Christ to suffer, and to rise from the dead the third day."

M. Suffering is often exaggerated in the Bible and termed "dead" as Paul said (1 Corinthians 15:31): "I protest by your rejoicing which I have in Christ, I die daily" (i.e. I suffer daily) (28).

By casting doubt upon the account of Jesus' disciples, which he calls "hearsay," Baagil tries to establish that the biblical text is corrupt. In using the word "dead" in a secondary meaning, he attempts to show that Christian interpretation is corrupted and mistaken. Baagil proceeds to assert that "on the cross" Jesus prayed that God would "remove this cup [of death] from me" (words Christ never spoke from the cross) and that God granted his request. After all, says Baagil, quoting Scripture, "The effectual prayer of a righteous man availeth much" (James 5:16 KJV).

Skilled Muslim apologists can rattle off Bible passages with an air of learning and sincerity that deceives many. Before twisting Jesus', James', and Paul's words to fit his diabolic doctrine, Baagil should have listened to another apostle, Peter, who wrote about Paul's letters, "His letters contain some things that are hard to understand, which ignorant and unstable people distort, as they do the other Scriptures, to their own destruction" (2 Peter 3:16).

A difficulty in dealing with tahrif is that one can never be quite sure of what aspect of it Muslims are talking about. Is part of the Bible still uncorrupted? If so, which part? When did this corruption take place—before or after Muhammad? How was it carried out? What happened to the "proto-Gospel"? Are there no copies of the correct text of the Bible? Muslims continue to use tahrif in various ways. Tahrif boils down to the contention that wherever the Bible and the Qur'an differ, either the Bible is wrong or the traditional interpretation of it is in error.

The Bible's Reliability

Muslims and others who reject Scripture point to numerous "errors" in the Bible. These errors can be classified in five categories: contradictions within the Bible, historical inaccuracies, scientific mistakes, moral errors, and mistakes in copying. We shall look at some examples of these problems and see how they might be resolved.

Contradictions are said to permeate the Scriptures. According to the book of Numbers, the Lord sent a plague upon the people of Israel because of their immorality: "Those who died in the plague numbered 24,000" (25:9). Recounting this event and using it as a warning for Christians, Paul wrote, "We should not commit sexual immorality, as some of them did—and in one day twenty-three thousand of them died" (1 Corinthians 10:8). The different numbers (23,000 and 24,000) are cited as a contradiction. This apparent contradiction between the Old and New Testaments can easily be resolved. One explanation might be that both writers used round numbers, with the exact figure somewhere in between. Another, albeit somewhat less likely, solution lies in Paul's use of the word *day*. Perhaps 24,000 died in the plague, 23,000 of them on one day and the rest on another.

Historical inaccuracies are another charge leveled against the Bible. For many centuries, critics of the Bible contended that Daniel chapter 5 contained a glaring historical error. Relating the famous handwriting-on-the-wall incident, that chapter speaks of a man named Belshazzar as the last king of Babylon. Yet according to historians, the last king of Babylon was Nabonidus, and there never was a King Belshazzar.

This problem has been resolved through modern archaeology. Although history had lost track of him, archaeological discoveries at Babylon have revealed Belshazzar's identity. According to the Babylonian archives, Belshazzar had ruled under his father Nabonidus. Before going on a lengthy expedition, Nabonidus had appointed Belshazzar king in his absence. So the Bible was right when it spoke of Belshazzar the King. This co-regency would also explain why Belshazzar could only make Daniel "the third highest ruler in the kingdom" (Daniel 5:16) (Arndt 81-2).

This example illustrates how some long-standing questions about Scripture have been resolved by modern archaeology. During the last century and a half, archaeological discoveries have brought to light many people (such as the Hittites) and places (such as Nineveh) that were mentioned in the Bible but denied by those who belittled Scripture's historical accuracy. The late Nelson Glueck, one of the world's most renowned archaeologists, said, "It may be stated categorically that no archaeological discovery has ever controverted [contradicted] a biblical reference" (McDowell 65).

What, then, did believers do before such discoveries? They simply adopted the attitude that with or without support from the outside, the Bible was right. This was their confidence in Scripture's inerrancy. Twenty-first-century believers share this attitude toward the Bible's few remaining historical difficulties.

Scientific mistakes are another indictment against Scripture. Joshua 10:13 contains what is perhaps the best known scientific "mistake" in the Bible: "So the sun stood still. . . . The sun stopped in the middle of the sky and delayed going down about a full day." Of course everyone today knows that the sun does not move across the sky. Rather, it is the earth's rotation that makes it seem as if the sun is moving. So if there was a miracle, it probably was not that the sun stood still but that the earth slowed in its rotation.

Even in today's scientific age, we speak of "sunrise" and "sunset." This is the natural way of describing the phenomenon, since from our viewpoint the sun does rise, move across the sky, and set. It is no more a scientific statement than when people speak of the "four corners of the earth." As for the miracle itself, that is a matter for faith.

Among the so-called *moral errors* of Scripture are some of the psalms that wish evil upon unbelievers. These are said to be contrary to the doctrines of love and forgiveness. Psalm 137:8,9, for instance, declares: "O Daughter of Babylon, doomed to destruction, happy is he who repays you for what you have done to us—he who seizes your infants and dashes them against the rocks."

Several things can be said here. First of all, the general tone of Scripture—both Old and New Testaments—does stress forgiveness. Furthermore, the Scriptures state that vengeance belongs to the Lord (Psalm 94:1). This does not, however, rule out the judgment of God. When people harden themselves in sin and unbelief, they are inviting judgment. This was the case with haughty Babylon, who had devastated many nations and had dragged God's chosen people, the Israelites, into exile. The psalmist was merely stating a fact of life—namely, that Babylon would reap what it had sown and that the children of Babylon would be dealt with as was the habit in war back then. Whoever would serve as the Lord's instrument of judgment is called "happy" (or "blessed"), because he would be doing God-ordained work.

As it turned out, the Persian Empire that overthrew Babylon also served as God's instrument for returning his exiled people to their homeland. All this was part of the divine and unstoppable plan that Christ might be born into the Jewish nation in the land of Israel. While the so-called imprecatory psalms invoke God's judgment, they do not call for a holy war.

Copying mistakes is the last category of errors. Before the invention of the printing press, all books, including the Bible and the Qur'an, had to be copied by hand. Some people claim that there are numerous mistakes in the handwritten copies, the manuscripts, of Scripture. It has been said that the New Testament alone contains thousands of copying mistakes. Since we no longer have the original texts of Scripture (written by Isaiah, Paul, Peter, etc.), skeptics contend that the many copying errors have left us with a greatly corrupted Bible.

Answering this type of accusation against Scripture is not especially difficult. There are over 14,000 ancient manuscripts of the Bible or portions of the Bible. This includes early translations as well as about five thousand Greek manuscripts from the New Testament. This amounts to about 13,000 more copies than of any other ancient book! The large number of manuscripts accounts for the huge number of errors sometimes attributed to the Bible. For instance, if in one early copy (let us call it copy "A") the words "Jesus Christ" were accidentally turned around (to "Christ Jesus"), that might affect two thousand other copies which were based on copy "A." In this way the same error would be multiplied two thousand times and be counted as two thousand errors. The variations that did creep into the different manuscripts are minor. The first variation in the New Testament is typical. Some manuscripts of Matthew 1:3 spell the name of one of Christ's ancestors *Zare* instead of *Zerah*.

Actually, only one-half of one percent of the New Testament text is affected by such copyists' error. To put it another way, the New Testament has about 20,000 lines; only in about 40 of those lines are we unable to decide for certain what the original said. Yet even though they do not make any teaching uncertain, Muslims will point to those few disputed passages in attempting to undermine the credibility of the entire Bible (Saal 100).

In addition, the existing manuscripts of Scripture (especially of the New Testament) date back extremely close to actual Bible times. Large portions of the New Testament predating the year 300 have been preserved. No other ancient writings can compare. For example, there are only about a dozen manuscripts of Julius Caesar's *Gallic War*. The oldest of them comes from about nine hundred years after Caesar actually lived and wrote. Yet no one questions the reliability of Caesar's history. Noted New Testament scholar Frederic Kenyon writes, "It cannot be too strongly asserted that the text of the Bible is certain. . . . This can be said of no other ancient book in the world" (McDowell 45). (See Geisler and Nix for a more thorough discussion of these textual concerns.)

As for the reliability of the Old Testament Hebrew text (which came to a close with the prophet Malachi's book some four centuries before Christ), the famous Dead Sea Scrolls have shown how reliable it is. Dating from before the time of Christ and predating other copies of the Old Testament by a millennium, the scrolls have substantiated the reliability of the text. Scholar William Green has summed it up, "[I]t may be safely said that no other work of antiquity has been so accurately transmitted" (McDowell 56). For this we can thank the scribes, who copied by hand the books of the Old Testament. In their desire for precision, they even counted the words and letters of each book to make sure they did not miss any.

A number of Muslim scholars are willing to concede these facts. Egyptian Muhammad Abduh says, "It would not have been possible for Jews and Christians everywhere to agree on changing the text. Even if those in Arabia had done it, the difference between their books and those of their brothers, let us say in Syria and Europe, would have been obvious" (Henry Martyn Institute 97). Turkish scholar Adil Ozdemir adds, "In my personal background I was led to believe that there are no more true Christians today who follow Jesus. I was also told that Christians changed their Scripture. If this had been true, then we might have proven how all this happened and why" (97).

Finally, when speaking of copying mistakes, it is always important to keep in mind that throughout the entire Bible *not one teaching is affected by copyists' errors.* As the numerous manuscripts attest, no other ancient book has been as carefully and accurately preserved. Statements about thousands of errors in the biblical manuscripts are grossly misleading.

The Bible's lofty status does not depend upon finding an answer to every difficulty. Even if there is some scriptural problem that believers have no answer for, it does not prove the Bible wrong. It only means our present knowledge is inadequate. Further research may come up with answers to the very few unanswerable objections raised against Scripture. Christians can be confident that the teachings in today's Bibles are no different from those in the original.

The Bible's Amazing Features

In addition to having withstood centuries of scrutiny and the onslaughts of unbelievers, the Bible has a number of amazing features that make it unique among the books of the world, including the Qur'an.

One of those features is *prophecy fulfilled.* The Old Testament Scriptures are full of predictions that are fulfilled in the person of Jesus Christ. For instance, the Old Testament prophets foretold that the Savior would be born in Bethlehem (Micah 5:2) and be preceded by a messenger (Isaiah 40:3). He would enter Jerusalem riding on a donkey (Zechariah 9:9), be betrayed by a friend (Psalm 41:9), be sold for 30 pieces of silver (Zechariah 11:12), and then this money would be used to buy a potter's field (Zechariah 11:13). He would be silent before his accusers (Isaiah 53:7), and his hands and feet would be pierced (Psalm 22:16). The probability of one man by chance fulfilling these eight prophecies is one in 10^{17}, that is, 1 in 100,000,000,000,000,000 (McDowell 167). Mere coincidence cannot account for what Jesus did. Without a doubt, the Christ of the New Testament is the same Savior of whom the Old Testament speaks.

In addition to prophecies fulfilled, the Bible has a distinctive *unity.* The Scriptures were written over a period of 1,500 years from Genesis, the first book of the Bible, to Revelation, the last. Nevertheless, a common thread runs through all those centuries and passes from the Hebrew Old Testament into the Greek New Testament. That unity or thread is the story of mankind's sin and God's forgiveness. The Old and New Testaments both point to Jesus the Christ, the God-man, who suffered for the sins of the world.

Moreover, the Bible has demonstrated an awesome *power* to touch individuals of all nationalities, classes, and occupations. Romans 1:16 describes this as "the power of God for the salvation of everyone who believes." The Bible not only has the power to make people recognize and repent of their sins, but it also has the power to bring sinners to trust in Christ the Savior.

Then there is the *beauty* of the biblical text. A person does not have to read or hear it in the original Hebrew or Greek to appreciate the Bible's literary greatness. The majestic simplicity of David's words continues to touch millions in the depths of their beings: "The LORD is my shepherd, I shall not be in want. He makes me lie down in green pastures, he leads me beside quiet waters . . ." (Psalm 23). Jesus' words echo that thought: "I am the good shepherd. The good shepherd lays down his life for the sheep" (John 10:11).

The imagery of Scripture's poetry and the grandeur of its narrative have never been surpassed.

Jesus and the Old Testament Scriptures

Christ's attitude toward Scripture is unambiguous. Without a doubt, Jesus considered it vital to one's very existence. Replying to the devil's temptation for Jesus to use his supernatural power for personal gratification, Jesus quoted the Bible, "It is written: 'Man does not live on bread alone, but on every word that comes from the mouth of God'" (Matthew 4:4). In contrast with Muslim divines, Christ did not cast doubt on the Old Testament, but he constantly attested to the veracity of the previous Scriptures.

Throughout his life on earth, Jesus demonstrated this complete reliance upon the Scriptures. He regularly went to the synagogues where he listened to and read the Bible. Fully one tenth of his recorded words are quotes from the Old Testament or references to it. Even his anguished cry from the cross "My God, my God, why have you forsaken me?" was quoted from Psalm 22. Christ accepted the Scriptures' claim of being God's Word. "Have you not read what God said to you?" Jesus asked in reference to an Old Testament passage (Matthew 22:31). Christ's regard for Scripture is summed up with his statement, "The Scripture cannot be broken" (John 10:35). It is inerrant.

After his resurrection, Jesus appeared to two disciples "and beginning with Moses and all the Prophets, he explained to them what was said in all the Scriptures concerning himself" (Luke 24:27). Thus Jesus continually declared himself to be the fulfillment of Old Testament prophecy. He also taught that the Old Testament sacrificial system pointed to him. Jesus said, "For even the Son of Man did not come to be served, but to serve, and to give his life as a ransom for many" (Mark 10:45). Furthermore, Christ used Old Testament history as a picture of himself. Referring to Numbers chapter 21, he stated, "Just as Moses lifted up the [bronze] snake in the desert, so the Son of Man must be lifted up, that everyone who believes in him may have eternal life" (John 3:14,15).

Christ expressed his relationship to Scripture when he said to the Jews, "You diligently study the Scriptures because you think that by them you possess eternal life. These are the Scriptures that testify about me" (John 5:39). With these words, Jesus proclaimed that *everything* in the Old Testament—prophecies, sacrifices, history—points toward him. No where does Muhammad make such dramatic claims.

The New Testament Scriptures

Toward the end of his ministry, Jesus told his disciples, "But the Counselor, the Holy Spirit, whom the Father will send in my name, will teach you all things and will remind you of everything I have said to you. . . . I have much more to say to you, more than you can now bear. But when he, the Spirit of truth, comes, he will guide you into all truth" (John 14:26; 16:12,13). With such words, Jesus promised his apostles that they, like the Old Testament prophets, would be inspired by the Holy Spirit. The men who received this promise and wrote the New Testament were Christ's disciples (such as Peter and John), men who worked and traveled with the disciples (such as Mark and Luke), and Paul, who received a special direct call from Jesus (Acts 9).

Like Jesus, the New Testament writers held the Old Testament in highest respect, referring to all but four of the Old Testament books: Ruth, Ezra, Ecclesiastes, and Song of Songs. These four are not excluded because they were not considered inspired but simply because there was no occasion to refer to them. They were definitely a part of the Scriptures in Christ's day. Since some references to the Old Testament books are not direct quotes, it is not easy to determine how many times the New Testament refers to the Old. It is safe to say that it is over five hundred times. While there are a few difficult transitions from the Old Testament to the New, there are none of the overwhelming problems in the New Testament that occur in the Qur'an's use of the Bible.

The New Testament writers were aware that their own writings were inspired. For instance, 2 Peter 3:1,2 places the apostolic writings on the same level with the Old Testament: "Dear friends, this is now my second letter to you. . . . I want you to recall the words spoken in the past by the holy prophets and the command given by our Lord and Savior through your apostles." In 1 Timothy 5:18, Paul quotes from the New Testament (Luke 10:7) and refers to it as "the Scripture."

Already in the lifetimes of the apostles, collections were being made of their writings. Peter spoke of "all" Paul's epistles (2 Peter 3:16), indicating that Paul's letters were being gathered. Paul himself encouraged this. He wrote to the Christians at Colosse, "After this letter has been read to you, see that it is also read in the church of the Laodiceans and that you in turn read the letter from Laodicea" (Colossians 4:16). The letter from Laodicea may be a reference to Paul's letter to the Ephesians in circulation.

As time went on, more and more books were collected in various areas. Before the year 200 almost every church came to possess the four gospels, Acts, 13 letters of Paul (Romans–Philemon), 1 Peter, and 1 John. The other seven New Testament books did not become widely used so quickly. It was not until A.D. 367 that all 27 books were mentioned together. This was in a listing by the great church father Athanasius.

The time span from the apostles to the first listing of the New Testament canon is not as great as it seems. All the books were recognized as authentic and were used in many places from the day they were written. Furthermore, the early Christians had no urgent need to draw up lists, and they had no central place to gather their Scriptures. The New Testament writings were scattered throughout Palestine, Asia Minor, Greece, and as far as Rome. This was very unlike the Old Testament era when worship constantly gravitated toward Jerusalem. Considering the distances separating the early churches, it is amazing that Christians everywhere today should have the same 27 books in the New Testament canon. The point is that the New Testament had been established well before the time of Muhammad.

The unity and gathering of the New Testament canon is all the more amazing in light of other literature that was also circulating in the ancient churches. There were several dozen "gospels," "epistles," and "revelations." The apostles had to contend with false teachers who would go so far as to write letters in the apostles' names. This had happened in the Thessalonian congregation. Someone had written that church in the name of Paul and had said that the end of the world was at hand. Paul corrected the misguided Thessalonians and told them "not to become easily unsettled or alarmed by some prophecy, report or letter supposed to have come from us, saying that the day of the Lord has already come" (2 Thessalonians 2:2). To prove the authenticity of his letter, Paul affixed his own signature at the end (2 Thessalonians 3:17). From the time of the apostles on, authentic, canonical, inspired material was distinguished from the false.

Over two thousand times, the Bible—Old and New Testaments—uses expressions such as "this is what the Lord says." Certainly such a book is worthy of consideration. Scripture declares the stakes are high—each person's eternal destiny. The Holy Spirit, working through the Word, brings people to the conviction that this is God's Word—"faith comes from hearing the message" (Romans 10:17).

The Divinity of Jesus and the Trinity

The Bible is a reliable foundation, but what about the teachings of Christ's divinity and the Trinity? Are these doctrines in the Scriptures, or have Christians erroneously read them into the Bible? These are more topics about which entire books have been written. Our discussion will be cursory.

The early years of Islam found John of Damascus (ca. 650–700) debating with Muslims the divinity of Jesus Christ, "the most delicate topic in a Muslim-Christian dialogue" (Sahas 79). That debate continues. Muslims have consistently ridiculed the notion that God could have a Son. Yet the Bible uses the word *son* in other ways besides meaning a physical male child who is the product of sexual union. The term *son* refers to one who has certain characteristics. Barnabas, for example, means "son of encouragement," not because Encouragement was his father's name, but because that was his nature. The Hebrew expression "son of man" is generally simply rendered "man." Zechariah 4:14 refers to "sons of fresh oil" (Hirji-Walji and Strong 126). That means they were priests who were involved in anointing. Similarly, the Bible speaks of those who are suffering as sons of affliction (Proverbs 31:5), those with tempestuous natures as sons of thunder (Mark 3:17), and so on.

In having the special designation the Son of God, Jesus is "in very nature God" (Philippians 2:6). Believers become "sons of God through faith in Christ Jesus" (Galatians 3:26). But only Jesus is *the* Son of God, as he himself put it, the "only begotten" or "one and only" (Greek: *monogenes*) Son of God (John 3:16).

Muslims point to passages in the gospels in which Jesus speaks of his humanity. As a man, he was born, grew up, ate and drank, was hungry and thirsty, spoke of the Father as "greater than I" (John 14:28), and died. Yet Jesus also referred to himself as God. In stating, "Before Abraham was born, I am" (John 8:58), Jesus was making a clear reference to the name by which God called himself when he spoke to Moses, "I AM WHO I AM" (Exodus 3:14). Jesus said to his disciples, "Anyone who has seen me has seen the Father" (John 14:9).

In resisting the temptation to worship the devil, Jesus quoted Scripture, "For it is written: 'Worship the Lord your God, and serve him only'" (Matthew 4:10). Nevertheless, there were many times when people "worshiped" Jesus, and he never corrected them. On one such occasion, "a ruler came and knelt before him" (literally, "worshiped him"), asking Jesus to raise his daughter who had just died. Jesus responded to the man's worship and raised the girl (Matthew 9:18-26).

The Old Testament foretold that the Messiah would be more than a mere man. To cite but one passage: "For to us a child is born, to us a son is given, and the government will be on his shoulders. And he will be called Wonderful Counselor, Mighty God, Everlasting Father, Prince of Peace" (Isaiah 9:6). Though Christ's kingdom is not worldly, it is eternal: "Of the increase of his government and peace there will be no end" (verse 7). Both Old and New Testaments speak of the Messiah in divine terms, as when, for example, he is referred to as Immanuel, "God with us" (Isaiah 7:14; Matthew 1:23).

As for the Trinity, the Bible emphatically states, "Hear, O Israel: The LORD our God, the LORD is one" (Deuteronomy 6:4), a passage Jesus quotes approvingly (Mark 12:29). At the same time, Scripture speaks of a plurality within the Godhead already in Genesis chapter 1. When God created the heavens and the earth, "the Spirit of God was hovering over the waters" (1:2). The Hebrew word for God, *Elohim,* is plural, even though it uses a singular verb. Thus God says, "Let us make man in our image, in our likeness" (1:26). This is not merely a "majestic plural," for the Old Testament does not support that use elsewhere. When Abraham was about to sacrifice Isaac, the Bible says, "[T]he angel of the LORD called out to him from heaven, . . . 'Do not lay a hand on the boy. . . .

Now I know that you fear God, because you have not withheld from me your son'" (Genesis 22:11,12). Here and elsewhere this special angel (messenger) of the Lord speaks both on behalf of God *and* as God. This divine "Angel" is the Son of God.

These same three persons appear in the New Testament: God the Father, the Son, and the Holy Spirit. Jesus brings everything together when he says, "All authority in heaven and on earth has been given to me. Therefore go and make disciples of all nations, baptizing them in the name of the Father and of the Son and of the Holy Spirit" (Matthew 28:18,19).

Muhammad in the Bible

Frequently Muslims argue that the Bible foretold the coming of Muhammad. As the Old Testament prophesied the coming of a Messiah, so the Bible—both Old and New Testaments—foretold the coming of Muhammad. In an effort to show that Muhammad was foretold in the Bible, some Muslim writers stretch almost every verse that has been applied to Jesus and say it really points to Muhammad. For the most part, the Muslim appeal rests on two texts, one from the Old Testament (Deuteronomy 18) and one from the New Testament (John 14 and 16).

Deuteronomy chapter 18 speaks of a prophet that God would raise up, who would be "like" Moses and from among the Israelites' "brothers." This could not refer to Jesus, writes Jamal Badawi, because, among other things, Moses and Muhammad were both married, while Jesus was not, and Moses and Muhammad were both earthly leaders, while Jesus was not (*Muhammad in the Bible* 41).

Badawi says that "brothers" refers to the Ishmaelites, but in fact, the context of Deuteronomy uses the expression to refer *definitely* to the Israelites. On that basis alone, Muhammad is disqualified. Twice the book of Deuteronomy refers to those outside Israel as "brothers" (2:4-8; 23:7); these passages specif-

ically mention the descendants of Esau (Edom) and not
Ishmael. Deuteronomy's many other references to "brothers"
are clearly to fellow Israelites. To refer back to Genesis (16:12;
25:18), which speaks of the "hostility" of Ishmael and his
descendants toward "all their brothers" (including no doubt
the descendants of Isaac) and to claim, as does Badawi, that
this somehow relates to the Deuteronomy chapter 18 passage is
to twist and distort the Scriptures.

As for the likeness to Moses, a few similarities bear mentioning. Both Jesus and Moses performed miracles. Both were
miraculously preserved in infancy from a pogrom to destroy
all infant boys. Both came out of Egypt (compare Exodus 2
and Matthew 2).

The lynchpin on which the case for Muhammad in the Bible
depends is John chapters 14 and 16. This section of the Bible
holds the key, if indeed Muhammad fulfills the Scriptures. The
Qur'an says, "And when Jesus son of Mary said: O children of
Israel Lo! I am the messenger of Allah unto you, confirming
that which was (revealed) before me in the Torah, and bringing
good tidings of a messenger who cometh after me, whose name
is the Praised One. Yet when he hath come unto them with
clear proofs, they say: This is mere magic" (Sura 61:6). Here is
the most direct statement Muhammad himself made about fulfilling prophecy.

The word for "Praised One" in Arabic is *Ahmad,* a variation of the name Muhammad. In John chapters 14 and 16,
Jesus promised the coming of the Holy Spirit, the Comforter
or Counselor. The Greek word for *Counselor* is *paracletos,*
which sounds like another word that means praised (Saal 66-
7). Muslims have charged that Christians altered the text. No
such evidence exists, and given the multiple copies of John's
gospel, such tampering could not have been carried out.
Muhammad's key reference to fulfilling the Scripture fails.

Some Muslims have taken another tack, appealing to an
extra-biblical source. Like modern liberal theologians,

Muslims have asserted that somehow the church excluded the true scriptures. Members of the so-called Jesus Seminar who have set out to establish the true text of the New Testament, including the addition of later apocryphal works, have been adequately refuted by scholars such as Philip Jenkins in *Hidden Gospels: How the Search for Jesus Lost Its Way*. Meanwhile, Muslims have appealed to the Gospel of Barnabas, which supposedly confirms the Qur'an and refutes the Bible. In reality it does neither. Even the Muslim *The New Encyclopedia of Islam* concludes, "[T]here is no question that [the Gospel of Barnabas] is a medieval forgery" (Glassé 78). It was written about 1300, in the wake of the Crusades.

In the higher-critical Muslim attacks upon Scripture, the Bible is its own best defense. The canonical books of Scripture have withstood severe negative criticism, and the person of Jesus Christ continues to tower above all others who have lived upon this earth. There is every reason to have confidence in him who "was delivered over to death for our sins and was raised to life for our justification" (Romans 4:25).

10. Witnessing to Muslims

Much of our study has been concerned with who's right. This is of fundamental importance. It would be foolish and even evil to want to share a falsehood with others. And it is of vital importance in discussing religion with Muslims, since they are taught that they have the final truth and that Christians are deluded.

Does it make a difference? Many would shrug their shoulders and say, "No." The obvious comeback, of course, is to ask whether it makes a difference if sincere believers in a cause fly airplanes into buildings and kill thousands of innocent people. On another level, does it make a difference if people are giving their lives to a lawgiver whose only assurance is do your best or if they live for the one who conquered death and who promises, "Because I live, you also will live" (John 14:19)?

The Bible teaches two great doctrines, the law and the gospel. The law tells us what to do, and in that function it makes us aware that we have not lived up to God's perfect standards. The gospel tells us what God has done for our salvation. Both need to be proclaimed. But before that, the question arises as to whether or not Christians should be witnessing at all.

God's Great Exchange

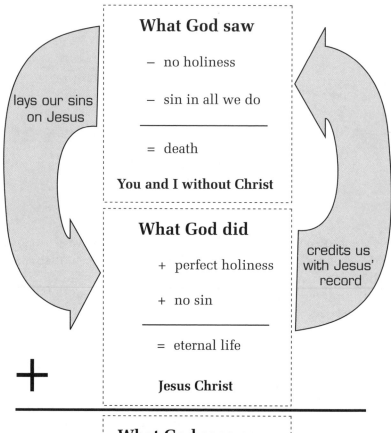

What God saw

– no holiness

– sin in all we do

———————————

= death

You and I without Christ

What God did

+ perfect holiness

+ no sin

———————————

= eternal life

Jesus Christ

+

What God sees now

+ perfect holiness

+ no sin

———————————

= eternal life

The new man in Christ

lays our sins on Jesus

credits us with Jesus' record

While It Is Day

Some would say that it is wrong to evangelize. I recall years ago, while still a seminary student, being angrily told by a Peace Corps worker in Iran that it was evil for missionaries to come and try to convert people to Christ. That continues to be the attitude of many. While criticizing missions in general, a recent article by Barry Yeoman focused on the practice of "contextualization," that is, blending into the culture of Islamic (or other) countries, offering medical and humanitarian services, and then sharing the Bible.

After commenting on the 2001 killings of 16 Christians by Muslim radicals in Pakistan, Yeoman immediately goes on to quote from a spokesman of the Council on American-Islamic Relations: "The issue is the disproportional power relationship. . . . They [Christians] use their resources to coerce people to do what they want them to" (47-8). Citing as an example a missionary group that offered veterinary services for impoverished cattle herders, the source continues, "You don't get the veterinarian unless you take the missionary" (48). The implication is that they had it coming. Especially faulted is the fact that in converting people to Christ, missionaries put the converts' lives in danger: "Missionary work often puts local believers in serious danger. . . . [In one country] significant numbers of Muslim-background believers were arrested and tortured due to their relationship to the expatriate missionaries" (49).

Jesus often told his followers that they would face persecution. The first Christians knew what it was to suffer for their faith; they also knew that it would bring earthly suffering to those who came to faith. "Do not be surprised," wrote John, "if the world hates you" (1 John 3:13). Yet John and the other apostles went out and preached, endangering their own lives and the lives of those who became Christians. None of this is to make light of suffering. We shudder at the very thought, and our hearts go out to those who endure persecution.

Ultimately, Christianity is not about leading a comfortable life in the here and now, a fact that is difficult for American Christians to grasp, having so long enjoyed the freedom to worship and practice our faith. Paul, a man who knew about being persecuted in numerous ways and places, wrote, "I consider that our present sufferings are not worth comparing with the glory that will be revealed in us" (Romans 8:18).

Aside from the issue of persecution, many mainline Christian denominations no longer have an interest in mission work largely because they have abandoned the ideas that Jesus is the only way to heaven and that the Christian faith is superior to other religions. "Live and let live" is supposedly the considerate way to relate. Is it considerate, however, to withhold sharing what is worthwhile and even of priceless value? There is a difference between sharing and trying to force one's beliefs on another. Jesus tells us that if others reject our message, we are simply to move on.

Ironically, at a time when Muslims are taking a renewed interest in missions, Christians are pulling back from missions: "As Muslims started developing missionary activities, Christians were shifting their focus from missionization to dialogue" (Busse 157). These Muslim activities include plans to place copies of the Qur'an in every hotel room (and every household!) in Japan, as well as to fortify missionaries with "intensive English classes" in preparation for work in western Europe and North America (157).

Christian outreach to Muslims, however, is not a matter of competition. Rather, it is a desire to carry out the Great Commission that Jesus has given to his church. After he rose from the dead and before he ascended into heaven, Jesus declared, "Go into all the world and preach the good news to all creation" (Mark 16:15). Elsewhere, Jesus urges us to seize the day of opportunity, which is today. Christ says, "As long as it is day, we must do the work of him who sent me. Night is coming, when no one can work" (John 9:4). In spite of all its daunting challenges, this is a time of wonderful opportunities in working among Muslims. For the past two decades, missionaries have been reporting breakthroughs in working among Muslims. Even in Saudi Arabia people are coming to faith in Christ and forming underground churches, thanks to radio broadcasts into the country (Guthrie).

With the influx of foreign Muslims into North America, Christians have opportunities to share the love of Christ with their neighbors. American newspapers carry stories about Christians converting to Islam. A *Milwaukee Journal* (now the *Milwaukee Journal Sentinel*) article several years ago spoke of the joy a number of area residents had found since their conversion to Islam (Rohde). The reverse does not seem so easy to find—not because it does not happen, but because it is not as socially polite. In fact, many Muslims are open to hearing about Christ.

In Muslim countries, the day of evangelizing seems to have given way to night. The Qur'an states, "The only reward for those who make war upon Allah and His messenger and strive after corruption in the land will be that they will be killed or crucified, or have their hands and feet on alternate sides cut off, or will be expelled from the land. Such is their degradation in the world, and in the Hereafter theirs will be an awful doom" (Sura 5:33). Abdullah Yusef Ali and M. H. Shakir translate "corruption" as "mischief." Christian missionary activity among Muslims would fall in that category.

The early lands of Christianity are now dominated by Islam. In a sermon, Luther likened the movement of the gospel to a passing thunderstorm:

> The Gospel is rather like a pelting rain that hurries on from place to place. What it hits it hits; what it misses it misses. But it does not return nor stay in one place; the sun and heat come after it and lick it up. Experience also teaches us that in no section

of the world has the Gospel remained pure and
unadulterated beyond the memory of a man. On
the contrary, it stood its ground and flourished as
long as those remained who had brought it to the
fore. But after they had passed from the scene, the
light also disappeared. Factious spirits and false
teachers immediately followed. (*What Luther
Says* 2:573)

Could it happen in our land? It's happening right now. Along
with the preaching of Christ across the land, God has richly
blessed America in every way. But people grow indifferent.
The man or woman down the street knows all about the latest
fads of fashion or entertainment. But how many people can
give half of the Ten Commandments or name even two of the
four evangelists—Matthew, Mark, Luke, John—who bring us
the great news of the life, death, and resurrection of the Son
of God?

The moment is fleeting. The task is daunting. The naysay-
ers are many. But from the distance comes the voice first
heard by Isaiah in the temple, "Whom shall I send? And who
will go for us?" (Isaiah 6:8). To which the prophet answered,
"Here am I. Send me!"

Proclaiming the Law and the Gospel

Witnessing to Muslims includes speaking both the law
and the gospel in love. The law and the gospel are the two
great doctrines that run through the Bible from Genesis to
Revelation.

The law declares what God's will is. It includes his commands—all the things we are to do or not to do in thought,
word, and deed. Jesus points out that the law includes inward
motivations as well as external acts. In the Sermon on the
Mount, for instance, Jesus declares:

You have heard that it was said to the people long ago, "Do not murder, and anyone who murders will be subject to judgment." But I tell you that anyone who is angry with his brother will be subject to judgment. . . .

You have heard that it was said, "Do not commit adultery." But I tell you that anyone who looks at a woman lustfully has already committed adultery with her in his heart. (Matthew 5:21-28)

This is the law, and Jesus sums it up when he says, "Be perfect, therefore, as your heavenly Father is perfect" (Matthew 5:48). While Jesus speaks of God as our Father in that passage, it is not with the same intimacy as when he says, "I and the Father are one" (John 10:30). Yet he does take on the authority of much more than a prophet, making his remarks not with the customary, "The Lord says . . ." but simply with, "I tell you . . ."

Jesus is the Lord, and he shows that God's law—his law— demands perfection. But the law does more than demand perfection, it also sets forth the wages of breaking it, the judgment. While Jesus is showing us how to live, he is also making it clear that we cannot perfectly fulfill the law.

Nowhere does the Bible say that good intentions are sufficient. "I did my best" is not enough. That is where the gospel comes in. The dictionary points out that the word *gospel* is from the Middle English word *godspel,* a term that means "good spell," "good story," or "good news." It is the same as the Greek word *euangelion,* evangel, which means "the good message" (the word *angel* means "a messenger").

So, what is the good news? It is simply that although we cannot fulfill the law, God has done it for us. Jesus summed up the gospel when he said, "God so loved the world that he gave his one and only Son, that whoever believes in him shall not perish but have eternal life" (John 3:16). Just as the law shows us what we are supposed to do and fail to do (it **S**hows **O**ur **S**in), the gospel shows what God has done for us—he sent his Son for our salvation (it **S**hows **O**ur **S**avior). In the gospel, there are no demands, no threats, no words of judgment. It is pure grace, undeserved love. "Come to me, all you who are weary and burdened," says Jesus, "and I will give you rest" (Matthew 11:28).

This is the same gospel in which Paul exulted. "I am not ashamed," he said in understatement, "of the gospel, because it is the power of God for the salvation of everyone who believes" (Romans 1:16). Believing is nothing more than taking what God freely offers: forgiveness, peace with God, the joy of salvation, and everlasting life.

Paul goes on to point out that this idea was nothing new when he adds, "Just as it is written: 'The righteous will live by faith'" (Romans 1:17). He is quoting from the prophet Habakkuk, but elsewhere, Paul goes back to Abraham himself: "Abraham believed God, and it was credited to him as righteousness" (Romans 4:3; Genesis 15:6). Abraham was righteous in God's sight. This was not because he was without sin—he was a sinner who twice offered his wife to other men. Rather, it was because Abraham simply trusted God's great promises: from him would come a great nation, his descendants would inherit the land, and "all peoples on earth will be blessed" through him (Genesis 12:3; 22:18).

Those blessings were not to come through the descendants of Ishmael, but through those of Isaac: "[Ishmael] will be the father of twelve rulers, and I will make him into a great nation. But my covenant I will establish with Isaac" (Genesis 17:20,21). As for the offspring or descendant through whom all nations would be blessed, Paul points out with the attention to detail so characteristic of the New Testament writers: "The promises were spoken to Abraham and to his seed. The Scripture does not say 'and to seeds,' meaning many people, but 'and to your seed,' meaning one person, who is Christ" (Galatians 3:16).

That one seed had been promised immediately after the fall into sin in the Garden of Eden when God spoke to the serpent: "I will put enmity between you and the woman, and between your offspring and hers; he will crush your head, and you will strike his heel" (Genesis 3:15). This was the first gospel promise, and it seems that Eve thought it might have been fulfilled already in the birth of her first child: "Adam lay with his wife Eve, and she became pregnant and gave birth to Cain. She said, 'With the help of the LORD I have brought forth a man'" (Genesis 4:1). The verse literally says, "I have brought forth a man the Lord." The words "with the help of" have been added in an attempt to get the sense of it. The literal rendering makes just as much sense. Eve thought that this son was the Lord—the divine, yet human, promised deliverer.

This talk about Jesus being the promised descendant, about Abraham believing and being counted righteous, about Adam and Eve being promised a Savior is talk that Muslims need to hear. They know the names of Jesus, Abraham, and Adam. But they do not know the gospel anymore than Muhammad knew it; and he (mis)used the gospel *(Injil)* as if it were a book handed down to Jesus.

Muslims, like all of us, need to hear both the law and the gospel. Without the law, we do not see how sinful we are and how much we need a Savior. Without the gospel, we are left in the hopeless condition of pleasing the holy God with flawed and utterly insufficient human efforts. The gospel without the law brings indifference. Why do I need this? The law without the gospel breeds either despair or a self-deceptive self-righteousness that fools no one, least of all the omniscient God who knows our every thought and deed.

Islam has a law. But it doesn't know the gospel. Driven by the law, the most devout Muslims will go to unbelievable lengths in the hopes of pleasing Allah, that distant god who has given a book but nothing of himself. There is a better way. We have to bring them the love of Jesus.

169

Proclaiming Christ

Only God knows how close and how ready some Muslims may be for the gospel. Although it is distorted and confused, they do have some knowledge of Jesus.

> Two small points may help a Muslim to believe Christ's death and resurrection. Jesus lived a fully human life; so it was natural for Him to go through the human experience of death (Hebrews 2:14,15). Secondly, according to the Qur'an, Jesus raised the dead; so, it should not be difficult for Muslims to believe that He Himself could rise from the dead, especially since the Bible so clearly states that He has risen from the dead. (Henry Martyn Institute 67)

Speaking the truth of the gospel in love through Jesus, we share God's undeserved gift of full and free salvation!

Islam in the United States

It is possible that some readers of this book have never met a Muslim. With the number of Muslims in North America at six million and growing, that is not likely to be the case a few years from now. The Bible has a wonderful message for Muslims, namely, that "true religion is more than good customs and ethical deeds" (Miller, "Love Thy Muslim Neighbor" 7). Salvation comes as a free gift through Christ alone. In the words of Peter, "Salvation is found in no one else, for there is no other name under heaven given to men by which we must be saved" (Acts 4:12).

Even if we do not now have the opportunity to witness, we can pray. The following passage from the gospel according to Matthew beautifully expresses the ongoing needs and opportunities; it also reminds us of the call to pray:

> Jesus went through all the towns and villages, teaching in their synagogues, preaching the good news of the kingdom and healing every disease and sickness. When he saw the crowds, he had compassion on them, because they were harassed and helpless, like sheep without a shepherd. Then he said to his disciples, "The harvest is plentiful but the workers are few. Ask the Lord of the harvest, therefore, to send out workers into his harvest field." (Matthew 9:35-38)

Some Dos and Don'ts

For reaching out to Muslims, here are some practical tips, ten dos and ten don'ts. For developing the material in this list, I am indebted to the two articles by Randy Duncan and to the anonymous book *Christian Witness among Muslims*.

> 1. Do know what the Bible teaches. Being well grounded in the faith is essential.

171

2. Do respect Muslims as people for whom Jesus died. The Bible says that "God was reconciling the world to himself in Christ, not counting men's sins against them" (2 Corinthians 5:19). The world includes everyone, and that reconciliation becomes each person's personal possession when he or she comes into a relationship of faith in Christ.

3. Do show sincere respect and friendship to Muslims.

4. Do listen to their real needs. Ask questions.

5. Do focus the conversation on Jesus Christ. Use the Word of God.

6. Do give literature about Jesus and the Bible.

7. Do invite a Muslim friend to a church service or to some function at church.

8. Do become well informed about Islam. This book is introductory. There is so much to learn. Books about missionaries to Muslims or Muslim converts to Christ are especially inspiring.

9. Do be available. We may not appreciate what a tremendous step it is for Muslims to convert. Even in North America, they face ostracism from their families and, especially in the case of Muslims from the Middle East, they live with the fear of physical reprisal and even death.

10. Do pray that Muslim hearts may be softened for the gospel. "Whatever good may be done is done and brought about by prayer," wrote Luther, "which is the omnipotent empress. In

human affairs we accomplish everything through prayer" (*What Luther Says* 2:1094).

1. Don't treat the Qur'an disrespectfully. It is one thing to disagree with the teachings of Islam, another to ridicule them.

2. Don't treat the Bible disrespectfully, by placing it on the floor, for example. Above all, don't undermine the Bible by ungodly living. It goes without saying that being a Christian means living by the Word as well as talking about it.

3. Don't get into a battle of the books—the Qur'an versus the Bible. It is important for Christians to understand the issues involved and to appreciate the reliability of the Bible. With that knowledge, let the Bible speak for itself. The straightforward assertions of the Bible are powerful, and through them the Holy Spirit works.

4. Don't make assumptions about what the Muslim believes. Ask him or her. In teaching the World of Islam course, it has been my experience that Muslims often are not that well informed about their own faith. On occasion, I have met people who claimed to be both Muslims and Christians at the same time.

5. Don't attack the name Allah as a false god. This is a touchy issue, since many Arabic-speaking Christians use the name Allah to refer to the God of the Bible. At the same time, an authority such as Robert Morey points out that the very name Allah is related to the pagan moon god of pre-Islamic Arabia.

6. Don't attack Islam, Muhammad, or the Qur'an. Duncan writes, "Few people have ever been debated into the kingdom. Light candles instead of cursing the darkness." Depending on their relationship to Islam, some Muslims may themselves be critical of the faith and ready to hear the other side.

7. Don't be insulting. It would be foolish to invite a practicing Muslim over for a pork dinner and wine. Other less obvious customs can be learned and watched. One is the practice of never holding the Qur'an below one's waist, because it would be insulting to do that. And since Muslims consider dogs to be unclean animals, keep your dog outside if a Muslim friend visits.

8. Don't witness alone to a person of the opposite sex.

9. Don't give up. St. Augustine's mother Monica prayed and witnessed for over a dozen years before her son became a Christian, and he became one of the greatest theologians of all time. (Luther was an Augustinian monk and learned much from him.)

10. Don't be afraid. It can be intimidating to share our faith—both for us and the other person(s) involved. Paul writes, "For God did not give us a spirit of timidity, but a spirit of power, of love and of self-discipline" (2 Timothy 1:7). Because of what Christ has done for us, we are confident God loves us, our salvation is certain, and Jesus is with us as we reflect his love and share it with others.

Various books on witnessing to Muslims offer a variety of approaches. One approach is that we begin with Christ in the Qur'an. In spite of its vociferous denials of the divinity and substitutionary death of Christ, in many ways the Qur'an speaks more highly of Christ than of Muhammad (see chapter 4). Look up the Qur'an's passages dealing with Christ (some editions have indexes in the back) and use them as links to the truth of the Bible.

Muslims Meet Christ

It has often been assumed that Muslims simply cannot change. There are too many obstacles: the ingrained idea they have that their revelation is newer and truer, the pressures of family and society, and even the fear factor that there will be physical retaliation if they convert. The fact is that, in spite of the difficulties, some Muslims do come to know Christ. An excellent book, *Unveiling Islam,* was written by two brothers who came to faith in Christ, even though it meant being disowned by their Muslim father. The long-time missionary to Muslims William McElwee Miller (1893–1993) wrote a moving book *Ten Muslims Meet Christ,* in which he describes the challenges facing those who become Christians in Muslim lands.

After years of closed doors and few converts, recent years have seen changes. In spite of persecution in Sudan, for example, the Christian church there "is growing fast with a great ingathering of people in the midst of terrible suffering through war, famine and persecution" (Guthrie 24). Even Saudi Arabia "where there were no known Christians only a few years ago—and where conversion from Islam to Christianity can be met with death—has a growing underground church" (24).

Some Muslims are turned off by the tactics of the terrorists. Many want more than the Qur'an has to offer. According to a survey among Muslims who became Christians, the biggest single motivation was "dissatisfaction with Islam. 'In the

Qur'an God forgives whom he wills and does not forgive whom he wills, so there's never assurance of salvation,' [the survey developer] writes. 'Generally, orthodox Muslims . . . have not felt close to God'" (Guthrie 24).

Sin keeps people from being close to God. Our study has shown that the Qur'an even urges Muhammad, "Ask forgiveness of thy sin" (Sura 40:55); yet nowhere does it mention sin in connection with Jesus. The Qur'an offers a fallible prophet who lies buried in Arabia. The Bible presents a sinless Savior who offered his life on the cross as a sacrifice for the sins of the world and who has conquered death.

Riccoldo da Montecroce wrote long ago, "The fact is: Christ lives, Muhammad is dead. A living advocate is better than a dead one" (114). Jesus Christ is our advocate, whose blood washes away our sins: "The blood of Jesus, his Son, purifies us from all sin" (1 John 1:7). Through the Word of God, the Holy Spirit brings us to saving faith: "No one can say, 'Jesus is Lord,' except by the Holy Spirit" (1 Corinthians 12:3). Now we are God's own children and can approach our heavenly Father in confidence and joy: "You are all sons [children] of God through faith in Christ Jesus" (Galatians 3:26).

This is a faith worth sharing. A friend of mine, a former Muslim from Iraq, says it most eloquently, "Allah calls on Muslims to sacrifice their sons so that they can go to paradise; God sacrificed his Son so that we can go to heaven."

A Final Word

At the time of this writing, the United States and other nations are involved in the War on Terrorism. In effect, it is a war on Islamic terrorists, the Islamicists. The greater war on terrorism is the struggle to free men, women, and children everywhere from the bondage to sin, death, and eternal destruction. This is not some sort of crusade of Christians *against* Muslims; rather, it is a crusade *for* Muslims. It is a battle against the satanic powers of false beliefs and false prophets, like Muhammad, who are enslaving people's minds and souls to gods that are not gods and ideologies that ultimately can bring no hope. It is a battle for people whom Jesus loves.

When all is said and done, Jesus Christ is the only real hope. He alone has conquered sin, Satan, and death. Rather than coming as some distant god, the bringer of more laws, he has come—and continues to come through the pages of the Bible—as our brother and closest friend. He has lived with us and for us, suffered and died for us, and promises, "I am with you always." In a word, he is *Immanuel,* "God with us."

Much more could be written on these matters than has been said in this volume. As important as the subject is and as much as is said about the politics, sociology, and economics involved, a relatively modest amount of information has been put into print that has a Bible-believing and Christ-centered focus. The discussions and debates will go on between the two world religions of Islam and Christianity. Although both, like Judaism, are rooted in the Middle East and are monotheistic religions, the divisions between them are deep, going back to their very sources, the Qur'an and the Bible.

While the differences cannot be ignored, they certainly need not be the cause of hatred or bloodshed. As both faiths continue to expand throughout the world, the years ahead promise to hold many more Christian-Muslim encounters. Wherever opportunities present themselves, this book is offered as a tool for Christians who use those opportunities to share their faith in Jesus. May we reach out to Muslims in a spirit of genuine concern and friendship, speaking the truth in love.

Soli Deo Gloria!

Questions for Study and Discussion

1. Muhammad and His Times

1. Why is it important to know some of the background of Islam?

2. What background knowledge of Islam did you have before reading this book?

3. What are the meanings of *Muslim* and *Islam?*

4. Discuss the religious setting of Arabia in Muhammad's day. Especially note the situation of Christians in the area.

5. What was the political setting of Arabia in Muhammad's day?

6. Muhammad was both a religious leader and a ruler. How does this contrast with Jesus?

7. What are your impressions of Muhammad the man? According to the prophet's wife Aisha, "He was a man just such as yourselves; he laughed often and smiled much. At home he would mend his clothes and cobble his shoes. He used to help me in my household duties; but what he did oftenest was to sew" (Shorrosh 50). How does this homey picture mesh with that of the warrior-prophet?

8. How did the Arab fascination with poetry and the spoken word find its culmination in the revelations of Muhammad?

9. What aspects of the historical background of Islam do you find especially interesting and valuable? How did Arabia compare with the land of Palestine, where so much Bible history took place?

2. Islam's Glorious Past

1. Why is the history of Islam vital for the understanding of Islam today?

2. In Muslim history there is little or no separation of church and state. How did Jesus lay the foundation for that separation among Christians?

3. What factors account for the rapid spread of Islam? Compare Islam's rapid spread with the early years of Christianity as recorded in the book of Acts.

180

4. In what ways is it possible to appreciate the Muslims' achievements in the arts, architecture, etc., while still not accepting their spiritual teachings?

5. What was the relationship of Martin Luther to Islam? How did his day parallel our own? How was it different?

6. How does the breakup of the Ottoman Empire almost a century ago still have major effects on the world today?

7. What aspects of Islamic history were new to you or did you find especially interesting?

8. The rapid spread of Islam—through Spain in the West and to India in the East within one hundred years—was spectacular. While the conquered people were not forced to become Muslim, they faced a heavy tax if they did not convert. They also had to be impressed with the conquests of Islam. What pressures and appeals might Islam have today as it continues to spread?

3. The Mosaic of Islam Today

1. When comparing major religions such as Christianity, Hinduism, and Islam, what great disunities do we find? How can those differences be approached?

2. Review the major movements in Islam—the Shiites, Sunnis, and Sufis.

3. Note the major differences between the teachings of the Baha'i faith and the Bible.

4. Many people judge the truth of a cause by the conviction of those holding it. The Bab died a martyr for the religion he founded. How did this affect the truth of his revelation? How might it affect people who are looking into Baha'ism?

5. Discuss the areas of Islamic strength throughout the world. What knowledge does the average American have of these areas?

6. How has oil contributed to the Islamic revival? What does the growth of Islam mean for world politics?

7. What recent news items—within the last week or so—can you recall that relate to Islam? What role does it play in the world, your country, and your community?

8. Islam continues to spread—quickly and quietly—already receiving rights denied to Christians in the land of the free. For example, in 2001, the New York City school system decided to allow prayer in school—"but only if you're a Muslim who wants to worship during Ramadan." Muslims even get their own prayer rooms in the schools (NewsMax). In 2002, the University of North Carolina decided to make a book containing portions of the Qur'an required reading for incoming freshmen and transfer students (Johnson). Whether such programs spread or not remains to be seen. What is the idea behind them? Why is it or why is it not fair?

4. The Qur'an

1. How does Muhammad's account of the revelation of the Qur'an by the angel Gabriel contradict the Bible?

2. Why do Muslims have no translations of the Qur'an but only interpretations?

3. Note some of the key features of the Qur'an.

4. If possible, get a copy of the Qur'an and do some reading in it. What are your impressions?

5. What were some of the sources of Muhammad's stories in the Qur'an? Why is it understandable that his accounts often differed from those in the Bible?

6. Simply given the fact that Muhammad lived 600 years after the Bible was complete (not to mention that he was removed in distance and language from the Bible lands), would it be natural to conclude that the more accurate source of information is the Qur'an or the Bible?

7. Read Jeremiah chapter 36. Here Jeremiah describes what it was like when God inspired him. How does his clear and certain dictation to the scribe Baruch differ from the way in which Muhammad uttered various passages of the Qur'an? In what way did Jeremiah's message change after the king burned the original scroll? (See verse 32.) How does this differ from the concept of Muhammad's abrogating or even forgetting previous utterances? What certainty did Jeremiah express, and what specific predictions did he make?

8. Muslims consider Jews and Christians "people of the book." The Qur'an supposedly builds on the Bible and offers a further revelation. Consider this in light of

Revelation 22:18,19. How does the Qur'an add to and take away from the book of Revelation, as well as the rest of the Bible?

5. Muslim Beliefs

1. Compare and contrast the Muslim belief in Allah with a biblical understanding of the nature of God.

2. Compare and contrast the Muslim beliefs of judgment, heaven, and hell with a biblical understanding of the nature of God.

3. Although Islam claims to honor Jesus, how does it really dishonor him? See John 5:22,23.

4. Many people think that beliefs are unimportant. Comment on this attitude.

5. What are the differences between Muhammad's concept of the devil and angels and that of the Bible?

6. At the heart of the difference between Islam and Christianity is the answer to how one is saved. Islam, like other religions, bases salvation on works. How did Jesus summarize the uniqueness of Christian faith in the most famous passage in the Bible, John 3:16?

7. Discuss any noticeable differences in the various translations of the Qur'an used in chapter 5. Unlike the Bible, the Qur'an does not have many lengthy narratives, but consists largely of short sayings, commands, and warnings. Does this make the Qur'an easy or difficult to follow?

8. What are the hadith? What role do they play in Islam?

9. How is Muslim belief irreconcilable with the Bible?

6. Muslim Practices

1. Review the five pillars of faith.

2. In what ways do the five pillars express the natural inclination of human beings to want to perform religious functions?

3. In what ways are the five pillars similar to Christian practices?

4. Comment on the observation of Henry Preserved Smith, writing more than a century ago: "But while we find some indications of a real spiritual apprehension of religion, it must be confessed that the emphasis of Mohammed is placed largely upon externals" (227).

5. With the emphasis on the performance of outward duties, how does Islam compare with the Pharisaic religion of Jesus' day?

6. In the face of terrorism and the reality of jihad, many insist that Islam is, at its core, a peaceful religion. Less than a month after 9/11, Oprah Winfrey used her hugely influential talk show to give the public a crash course in "Islam 101" and assert that Islam is "the most misunderstood of the three major religions" (Dreher) and basically peaceful. What kind of impressions are the popular media

trying to convey to the public? What kinds of impressions does the public have of Islam?

7. What are the stereotypes of Muslim attitudes toward women, and are they unfair? How do Muslim views compare with biblical teachings? See Ephesians 5:22-33; 1 Peter 3:1-7.

8. Islam is a religion of laws. Comment on that. Compare that with the Christian faith.

7. Islam and Christianity

1. Review the Crusades. What were the causes and the results of this historic episode?

2. What distinctions are there between the Crusades and the idea of defending ourselves against Muslim jihad (or any attack)?

3. Review some of the different attitudes toward Islam that you have come across in the news media or elsewhere.

4. What is the current situation for Christians in Muslim lands?

5. Muslim Pakistan and Hindu India have fought three wars since the partition of the two countries in 1947 (Duff-Brown). Discuss how such conflicts demonstrate that not all Muslim conflicts are with Christianity and Judaism.

6. Could Islam ever become the dominant religion in Europe or North America? What lessons does history teach?

7. What is the worldwide situation between Islam and Christianity today? How has it changed in your lifetime? Without trying to be a prophet, what do you think the future holds? What assurances does God's Word give? See, for example, Psalm 46; Matthew 28:19,20; Romans 8:28.

8. Islam Evaluated

1. Note some of the problems with the Qur'an. What are the satanic verses, and what is their significance?

2. Note some of the external problems with the Qur'an, such as its relation to history.

3. Note some of the internal problems, such as the doctrine of abrogation.

4. What are some of the obvious differences between the Bible and the Qur'an?

5. *The Encyclopedia of Islam* states matter-of-factly that "classical [Islamic] literature records thousands of variants, which, however, are not found in any extant manuscripts known to Western scholars" (Bosworth 404). Nevertheless, Muslim apologists (defenders) insist on the immutability (unchangeableness) of the Qur'an. Why is this so vital to Islam?

6. In what ways was the Arabian Christians' lack of biblical knowledge or ability to share it a tragedy that the world is still living with? How can Christians today learn from that history? What should be our attitude about the Bible and sharing it with others?

7. What aspects of the Qur'an were new to you? In what ways is the history of the Bible's formation much more complicated—and at the same time richer—than that of the Qur'an?

9. The Bible: God's Revelation

1. Review some of the Muslim (and higher critical) objections to the Bible.

2. Why is it important to understand something about textual criticism?

3. Consider this example of an Old Testament textual difficulty: The Bible calls King Nebuchadnezzar the father of King Belshazzar of Babylon (Daniel 5:18). Yet it is a historical fact that Nabonidus, not Nebuchadnezzar, was Belshazzar's father; Nebuchadnezzar was Belshazzar's grandfather. How might this historical problem be resolved? See Genesis 28:13.

4. Consider this example of a New Testament textual difficulty: Compare Matthew 27:44 with Luke 23:39,40. One passage speaks of one criminal hurling insults at Jesus; the other speaks of two doing it. How might this problem be resolved?

5. What is the Christian's attitude even if he or she cannot find the answer to some "error" in the Bible? What suggestions did St. Augustine offer when he wrote, "If, here or there, I stumble upon something [in the Bible] which seems not to agree with the truth, I make no doubt that either the copy is faulty, or the translator did not express exactly the thought of the original, or that I do not understand the matter" (Pache 157)? What does the fact that Augustine (354–430) addressed such issues tell us about many of today's concerns regarding Scripture?

6. Since history has seen the Bible vindicated against its attackers so often through the years, what confidence can this give 21st-century believers?

7. According to Deuteronomy 18:14-22, what would distinguish true spokesmen (prophets) of God from false ones?

8. Which comes first, trust in Jesus or trust in the Bible? In what ways are the two related to each other?

9. Scripture itself states that some parts of the Bible are more difficult to understand than others (2 Peter 3:15,16). What does this say about the need to study the Scriptures carefully and thoroughly?

10. In what ways is Jesus Christ far greater than the prophets and apostles of the Bible and the prophet of Islam, Muhammad?

10. Witnessing to Muslims

1. What are some things to keep in mind when sharing one's faith with Muslims?

2. What are some things to avoid in witnessing to Muslims?

3. What would you add to the list of dos and don'ts?

4. How does an understanding of Islam aid in a desire and an ability to reach out to Muslims?

5. Discuss why prayer is so important in reaching out to Muslims.

6. What opportunities are available in your community for evangelism to Muslims? What opportunities does your church present?

7. What role can you play in overseas outreach to Muslims?

8. Writing on the growth of Christianity in a Muslim area of Africa, Charles Edward White speaks of people becoming Christians through "the martyrdom of several believers" (40). What role does suffering play in the spread of the gospel?

9. Strongly Islamic countries, such as Saudi Arabia, are closed to Christian mission work, while the West is wide open to Muslim efforts. Yet Muslims are coming to Christ. What does this tell us about the power of the gospel? How

should it encourage us to support overseas missions, many of which encounter Islam? See Romans 1:16; 1 Corinthians 1:18-25; Colossians 2:2-4.

10. Why is love the key to reaching Muslims?

Vocabulary

Abbasids. the second major dynasty of the Islamic empire, which ruled from 750 until the conquest of Baghdad by the Mongols in 1258; Abbasid caliphs lost effective, centralized power from at least the early tenth century

abd. slave; common in names, e.g., Abdullah—slave of God

ablution. ritual washing to achieve a state of purity in connection with various significant events, such as before visiting a mosque or after contact with a dead body

abrogation. the setting aside of one revealed teaching by another later revelation

abu. father of; common in names, e.g., Abu Hamid

Abu Bakr. early companion (and father-in-law) of Muhammad; first caliph after the death of the prophet (632–634); consolidated the position of Islam in the Arabian Peninsula

A. H. "after Hijra," denoting years on Islamic calendar

Ahmad b. Hanbal. scholar of traditions (Hadith) who died in Baghdad in 855; founder of a school of religious law that emphasized the importance of traditions over reasoning; a hero to conservatives for his courageous stand against the caliph's attempt to impose the doctrine that the Qur'an was created

Aisha. daughter of Abu Bakr, wife of Muhammad

Ali b. Abi Talib. young cousin and son-in-law of the prophet Muhammad; raised in his household; fourth caliph

(656–661); the first imam of the Shi'is

Allah. Arabic word used by Muslims for God; literally, "the god"; often used by Arabic-speaking Christians for the tri-une God

amir (emir). ruler, commander, chief, nobleman

Ansar. the Helpers; a title given to the people of Medina who helped Muhammad and fought at his side

antinomian. one who opposes the authority of the law

apologist. a person who writes or speaks in defense of a doctrine or religion

arabesque. the distinctive decora-tive motif based on natural forms arranged in infinitely repeating geometric patterns; used in many forms of Islamic art after the tenth century

arbiter, arbitrator. one chosen or appointed to judge a disputed issue

arkan. pillars or supports; the five pillars of Islam are confes-sion, prayer, fasting, almsgiv-ing, and pilgrimage

ascetic. a person who leads a life of austere self-discipline and self-denial, especially as an act of religious devotion

ayah (aya). sign or symbol of God's power and mercy; single verse of the Qur'an

ayatollah. "sign of God," highest rank of Shiite Muslims

bab. door; used to refer to the door of private interpretation

Baha'ism. a world religion with its roots in 19th-century Shiite Iran; this religion seeks to com-bine all religions into one uni-versal faith

banu (bani). before a tribal name means "children of," e.g., Banu Quraysh

baraka. blessing

beduin (bedouin). an Arab of any of the nomadic tribes of the deserts of North Africa, Arabia, or Syria

bid'ah (bid'a). innovation, with the usual connotation of "deplorable"; something for which there is not authority in the practice of the prophet

Bismillah. "In the name of Allah," beginning of prayer recitation

burqa. a full-length woman's cloak with veil; a term used in south-ern Asia, notably Afghanistan

Byzantine Empire. the state cen-tered in Byzantium (formerly Constantinople, later Istanbul), growing out of the late Roman Empire in the fifth century A.D. and ending with the conquest of the capital by the Turks in 1453; one of the two major powers of the late antique Mediterranean world; offi-cially Christian since the con-version of Constantine

caliph (khalifa). "successor," "deputy," "substitute"; espe-cially the successor of the prophet as the leader of the community

calligraphy. the art form based on beautiful handwriting

chaddar (chador). a full-length woman's cloak with veil; a term used in Iran

Companions, Successors. the first and second generation of Muslims (Companions were in direct contact with Muhammad; Successors were in contact with the Companions)

dar al-harb. the abode of war, i.e., territory not under Muslim sovereignty, against which warfare for the propagation of Islam is licit; the converse of dar al-Islam, the abode of Islam

dar al-Islam. house of Islam; territory under Islamic sovereignty or areas where Islam is secure

darwish (dervish). a member of a mystical order; saintly person, mendicant

dhikr (zikr). "remembrance," especially applied to the Sufi group's practice of invoking or chanting the name of God

dhimmi. a member of one of the protected religions, i.e., the non-Muslim religions tolerated by the Muslim state in accordance with the shari'a, on payment of certain taxes and on acceptance of an inferior social status

Eid-ul-Adha. one of the two major holidays, the Feast of Sacrifice

Eid-ul-Fitr. one of the two major holidays, the feast of Breaking the Fast of Ramadan

falsafa. philosophy

fana'. "annihilation" in God, an aspiration of Sufis

faqih. a doctor of the shari'a; a canon lawyer of Islam

faqir (fakir). a member of a mystical order; dervish; poor man

Fatima. the daughter of Muhammad

Fatimids. Shiite Muslim dynasty in North Africa with its capital in Cairo, Egypt (969–1171); named after Muhammad's daughter Fatima

fatwa (plural, fatawa). an authoritative, advisory legal opinion issued on request by a specialist of the religious law

fiqh. "understanding," especially of the religious law; can refer to jurisprudence (the philosophy of law) or the positive law itself

Ghadir Khumm. resting place where Muhammad stopped on the return from his farewell pilgrimage, where Shi'is believe he designated Ali as his successor

hadith. a formal report of the sayings and deeds of the prophet Muhammad, containing his exemplary practice (sunnah); the second source of authority (after the Qur'an) in law, life, and theology for Muslims

hafiz. a Muslim who memorizes the Qur'an

hajj. annual pilgrimage to Mecca; prescribed at least once in a lifetime for all Muslims who are able; one of the five pillars of Islam

hajji. one who has performed the hajj

Hanafi. one of the four main schools of law of Sunni Islam, named after Abu Hanifa

Hanbali. one of the four main schools of law of Sunni Islam, named after Ahmad b. Hanbal

hanif. Qur'anic term for a true monotheist, such as the prophet Abraham, who worshiped one god while living in pagan times, and the worshipers of Allah in Arabia, who had already turned away from polytheism before the time of Muhammad

haram. that which is forbidden

al-Haramain. the two sacred sanctuaries of Mecca and Medina; Jerusalem is said to be the third sacred sanctuary

Haram al-Sharif. the Noble Sanctuary, Jerusalem

harim. female part of the household, to which non-related males are not admitted

Hasan. first son of Ali b. Abi Talib and Fatima; grandson of Muhammad; second Shiite imam; abdicated his caliphate to Muawiya

hijab. a woman's scarf or head covering

Hijaz. the western part of what is now Saudi Arabia, where Mecca and Medina are located

hijirah (hijra). migration of Muhammad and his followers from Mecca to Yathrib (later known as Medina) in A.D. 622, marking the beginning of the Muslim era

Husain (Husayn, Hussein). second son of Ali b. Abi Talib; third Shiite imam; killed by Umayyad forces at Karbala', sealing the split between the Sunnis and the Shi'is

hypostyle. having a roof supported on many columns

Iblis. Qur'anic name for the fallen angel, the devil

ibn (bin). son of; corresponds to Hebrew ben; often abbreviated b. in names, e.g., Ali b. Abi Talib

Ibrahim. the prophet Abraham; said to have built the Ka'abah with his son Isma'il

Id (eid). feast, holiday, festival; the two most important festivals are Id al-Adha, the Feast of Sacrifice, and Id al-Fitr, the Feast of Breaking the Fast of Ramadan

ijma'. "consensus," usually understood as that of legal scholars concerning a point of law; consensus of the community

ijtihad. "effort," especially the exercise of independent judgment in Islamic law to arrive at a fresh interpretation of a point at issue

ilm. "knowledge," particularly religious learning

imam. a prayer leader; the leader of the Muslim community; for Shi'is, the legitimate leader, Ali or one of his specially designated descendants, chosen by God as a sinless intermediary between him and the Muslims; the last one (seventh or twelfth) has been living in a state of occultation for some 1,000 years

immah (umma). the community of Muslims

Injil. the gospel; understood as a sacred book revealed to Isa (Jesus)

irhab. terrorism

Isa. Jesus; designated as Isa Nabi, Jesus the Prophet; Isa Masih, Jesus the Messiah; or simply as Jesus, the son of Mary, Ibn Maryam

Islam (Muslim). submission to the will of Allah; the religion of submitting to God's will; one who submits to and practices the religion of Islam

Islam. submission, i.e., to God

Isma'il. the prophet Ishmael; said to have built the Ka'abah with his father Ibrahim

Isma'ili. also known as Sevener; a minority tradition among the Shi'a; one of the two main groups of Isma'ilis, the Nizaris follow the Aga Khan as its Living Imam; the other group, the Mustalians, believes its Imam is in concealment

isnad. chain of transmitters or authorities prefixed to a hadith and guaranteeing its authority

iwan. a vaulted space open at one end; taken from the Persian tradition and often used in mosques, especially in arrangements of several iwans facing a courtyard

Jahiliyyah (Jahiliyya). "time of ignorance," a term applied in the Qur'an to the period of paganism before the coming of Islam

jihad. the duty of Muslims to struggle for the faith, including fighting unbelievers; holy war

jinn. demons or angels; created by God from fire and capable of assuming human or animal form

jizya. the poll tax paid by dhimmis

juma. assembly; the Juma prayer is the Friday congregational prayer

kafir. an infidel; an unbeliever; i.e., a non-Muslim

Ka'abah (Kaaba). the cube-shaped shrine in the center of the great mosque in Mecca, toward which all prayers are directed; contains the Black Stone, a meteorite considered holy and dated from pre-Islamic times; in pre-Islamic times, the Ka'abah held many idols

kalam. scholasticism; theology

Karbala'. site of the military engagement where Ali's second son Husain and his family were killed by Umayyad forces trying to prevent them from reaching supporters in Kufa

Khadijah (Khadija). Muhammad's first wife, a widow older than he who remained his only wife while she lived, who became the first person to accept Islam, and who supported Muhammad throughout his mission

khanqah. Sufi meeting place or lodge

kharay. land tax paid by dhimmis

Kharijites (Khawarij). the first sectarians in Islam, originating with those who "went out" (kharala) from Ali's camp when he accepted arbitration rather than the judgment of God in his battle with his Umayyad opponent (later, one of them was responsible for Ali's murder)

kiswa. the ceremonial drapery placed over the entire Ka'abah and renewed each year

kitab. book, scripture; al-Kitab is a synonym for the Qur'an

kiyas (qiyas). method of reasoning by analogy

madhhabis. the schools of jurisprudence

madrasah (madrasa). a medieval college for the teaching of law, often attached to a mosque; Islamic religious school

Magirib. Arabic-speaking countries of North Africa, west of Egypt

Mahdi. "the guided one"; in Shi'i belief, the last Imam, presently living in occultation, who will return at the end of time to fill the world with justice, as it is now filled with injustice, and whose appearance will signal the Last Judgment

malak. an angel

Maliki. one of the four main schools of law of Sunni Islam, named after Malik b. Anas

maqsura. a screened and often highly decorated area near the mihrab of a mosque, usually reserved for the ruler or his representative

Masihi. Christian; from al-Masih, the Christ, the Messiah

matn. the body or text of a hadith report (as distinct from its chain of authorities, or isnad)

mawali (singular, mawla). non-Arab Muslim

mawlid. celebration of the birthdays of Sufi figures or, especially, of the prophet

Mecca (Makkah). trading town that was the birthplace and first home of Muhammad; a cult center for surrounding tribes; later the focus of prayers and the pilgrimage destination for Muslims around the world

Medina (Yathrib). "City" of the Prophet; name given to the agricultural town of Yathrib, which welcomed Muhammad and his followers when they were forced out of Mecca; place where Islam assumed its final form, as a political as well as religious entity

mihrab. recessed space on the wall of a mosque showing the direction of Mecca, which believers face in prayer

minaret. tall tower attached to a mosque; often used to call the faithful to prayer

minbar. raised platform or pulpit in a mosque

monotheism. worship of a single deity

mosque (masjid). "place of pros-tration," a building for commu-nal prayer and other religious purposes of Islam

muezzin. the caller of the azan, or "summons to prayer"; when the mosque has a minaret, he calls from the top of it, but in smaller places of worship, he calls from the side of the mosque; the first muezzin was Bilal, the son of a black slave girl

mufti. the officer who expounds the law; he assists the qadi, (qazi) or judge, and supplies him with fatwas, or decisions; he must be learned in the Qur'an and hadith and in the Muslim works of law

mugarnas. tiers of niche-like units that project from the niche below; compared to sta-lactites and often used in tran-sitional design elements, such

as supports for domes; from the middle period on, they became very common in Islamic designs

Mughals. dynasty ruling in India from 1526 to 1858, the Mongols

Muhammad. Meccan orphan who lived from approximately A.D. 570 to 632, who became the founding prophet of Islam

mujahid. one entitled to give an independent opinion in legal matters or theology

mujahidun. soldier or warrior of Allah

mulla (mullah). a Muslim divine

Muslim. one who surrenders to Allah; a follower of Islam

muta. a temporary marriage for a stipulated time

nabi. prophet

naskh. abrogation; a term used to designate the abrogation of some verses of the Qur'an by others, or of previous scrip-tures by the Qur'an

Ottomans. major dynasty ruling much of the Middle East from 1281 to 1924, the Turks

pagan. a person who is not a Christian, Muslim, or Jew; hea-then; one who has no religion

pantheism. the belief that God is everything and everything is God

parda (purdah). curtain or veil; it may refer to women's seclu-sion or women's dress

polytheism. worship of many deities

qadi (kadi). a judge appointed by the ruler to decide cases according to the sharia

al-Qa'ida. the foundation, base; a model or principle, something one should aspire to follow

qiblah (qibla). the direction of Mecca (specifically, of the Ka'abah), which one faces in prayer

qiyas. analogy, especially in law

Quraysh (Quraish). the tribe of Muhammad, which controlled Mecca; in the Qur'an the tribe is denounced for its stubborn opposition to Islam, but the first two Islamic dynasties were of Qurayshi descent

Qur'an (Koran). literally "recitation," the speech of God to Muhammad that is the scripture of the Muslims

qussas. popular preachers who transmitted religious lore in a non-scholarly fashion in the early days of Islam

qutb. "axis" around which turns an invisible hierarchy of Sufis who assure the spiritual well-being of the world

al-Rabb. The Lord, a term applied to Allah

Ramadan. the month of the pre-scribed total fast (sawm) during daylight hours, one of the five pillars of Islam

rasul. messenger; apostle of God; usually applied to Muhammad

ra'y (rayi). human reasoning used as a source of law; free opinion in legal or theological matters

rihlah. "journey," for the pilgrim-age or especially for the pur-pose of collecting hadith or other religious study

Safavids. major dynasty ruling Persia (Iran) from 1501 to 1732

salat. canonical prayer or wor-ship; prescribed for Muslims five times daily; one of the five pillars of Islam

Sassanians. dynasty that ruled the Persian Empire (one of the two major powers of the late antique Mediterranean world) at the time of Muhammad; Zoroastrian in religion

sawm. fasting; one of the five pil-lars of Islam (*see* Ramadan)

Sevener. see Isma'ili

Shafii. one of the four main schools of law of Sunni Islam, named after Muhammad b. Idris al Shafii (767–820), widely known as the Father of Islamic Jurisprudence

shahadah (shahada). "witness," the Muslim profession of faith ("There is no god but God and Muhammad is the messenger of God"); one of the five pillars of Islam

shaikh (shaykh). "elder"; leader of a tribe; a learned, pious man or teacher; a Sufi mentor

shari'ah (shari'a). the will of God, as expressed in the religious law of Islam

sharif. notable person, a descendant of Muhammad

Shaytan. Satan

Shi-ah. the "party" of Ali, who evolved a distinct understanding of the Islamic faith

Shiite (Shi-is). Muslim of the party of Ali

shirk. polytheism; cardinal sin of associating something with God in worship, or of worshiping something other than God

Sufi. a Muslim mystic

sunnah (sunna). "trodden path"; tribal custom of pre-Islamic Arabs; usually refers to the normative practice of the prophet, as seen in the hadith reports

Sunni. one who adheres to the practices and the understanding of the faith of the majority Muslim community, not rejecting the legitimacy of the first three caliphs in favor of Ali

surah (sura). one of the 114 chapter divisions of the Qur'an

tahrif. corruption of the scriptures; applied by Muslims to Jews and Christians in regard to the Bible

tariqah (plural, tariqat). the Sufi "I path"; a Sufi brotherhood

tawhid. Allah's complete and total oneness; a denial of the Trinity

tiraz. "embroidery"; inscribed fabrics made in state workshops and distributed as rewards or marks of favor by rulers; by extension, the writing embroidered on (or woven into) the fabrics

Twelver. the group of Shi'is who accept a line of twelve (rather than seven) divinely selected Imams who have guided the community

ulama' (singular, alim). the group of scholars trained in the religious law

Umar. an important companion of the prophet and the second caliph of Islam (634–644), who very skillfully guided the early conquests and administration of much of western Asia and North Africa

Umayyads. a clan of the Quraysh tribe; first hereditary dynasty of the Islamic empire, ruling from Ali's death in 661 until they were replaced by the Abbasids in 750

umm. Mother; often used in names, e.g., Umm Ahmad (mother of Ahmad)

ummah (umma). the worldwide community of Muslims

Uthman. an aristocratic Meccan and early companion of Muhammad who became the third caliph of Islam (ruled 644–656); he was accused of mismanagement and of giving too much latitude to his

Umayyad relatives; his successor Ali, in turn, was accused of insufficient vigor in pursuing Uthman's murderers

Wahhabi. fundamentalist Muslim movement, especially influential in Saudi Arabia

wali Allah. "friend of God," or Sufi holy person who enjoys a special relationship with God

warp. the threads that run lengthwise on a fabric (and must be carefully placed on the loom), crossed at right angles by the woof, or weft; carpets have played an important economic role in Muslim history

weft. the horizontal threads interlaced through the warp in a woven fabric, often in complicated patterns; carpets have played an important economic role in Muslim history

wudu. ablution before Muslim prayer

Yathrib. original name of Medina, the agricultural town that welcomed Muhammad and his followers when they were forced out of Mecca

Zabur. writing; the psalms revealed to the prophet David

zakat. obligatory alms or "purification tax" paid by Muslims; one of the five pillars of Islam

zina. adultery, fornication

zindiq. dualist; heretic

Bibliography

Abdul-Haqq, Abdiyah Akbar. *Sharing Your Faith with a Muslim.* Minneapolis: Bethany Fellowship, 1980.

Ahmad, Kassim. *Hadith: A Re-evaluation.* Tucson: Monotheist Productions International, 1997.

Albrecht, Mark. *Lutheran Orient Mission Society Messenger.* Vol. 92, No. 3 (May-June 2003).

Ali, Abdullah Yusef, trans. *The Qur'an.* Elmhurst, NY: Tahrike Tarsile Qur'an, 2002.

Anderson, M. *The Trinity: An Appreciation of the Oneness of God with Reference to the Son of God and Holy Spirit for Christians and Muslims.* Caney, KS: Pioneer, 1995.

Andrae, Tor. *Mohammed: The Man and His Faith.* Translated by Theophil Menzel. New York: Harper & Row, 1960.

"Arabia: The Countries of Arabia: Saudi Arabia: History: The Wahhabi Movement." *Britannica Online.* www.eb.com:180/cgi-bin/g?DocF =macro/5000/24/64.html.

Arberry, A. J. *Aspects of Islamic Civilization as Depicted in the Original Texts.* Ann Arbor: University of Michigan Press, 1967.

___, trans. *The Koran Interpreted.* New York: Touchstone, 1996.

Archer, Gleason L., Jr. "Anachronisms and Historical Inaccuracies in the Koran." Appendix 2 in *A Survey of Old Testament Introduction.* Chicago: Moody, 1985.

Armstrong, Karen. "Ghost of our Past: To understand the war on terrorism, we first need to understand its roots." *Modern Maturity.* (January-February 2002), pp. 44-7,66.

Arndt, W. *Bible Difficulties.* St. Louis: Concordia, 1971.

Baagil, H. M. *Christian Muslim Dialogue.* Saudi Arabia: Islamic Da'awa & Guidance Center, 1984.

Badawi, Jamal. *Muhammad in the Bible.* Plainfield, IN: Muslim Students' Association of the United States and Canada, 1982.

___. *The Status of Women in Islam.* Indianapolis: Muslim Students' Association of the United States and Canada, 1972.

___, and John Brug. *Who is Jesus?* Videotape and notes of a Christian-Muslim debate held at the University of Wisconsin–Milwaukee, April 4, 1989.

Bailey, Richard P. "Jihad: The Teaching of Islam from Its Primary Sources—the Qur'an and Hadith." 1996. www.answering-islam.org/Quran/themes/jihad.htm.

Barnstorne, Willis, ed. "Basilides." *The Other Bible.* San Francisco: Harper & Row, 1984, pp. 626-34.

Bat Ye'or. *The Dhimmi: Jews and Christians under Islam.* London: Associated University Presses, 1985.

BBC News. "'Biblical Temple' tablet found." (January 14, 2003). http://news.bbc.co.uk/l/hi/world/middle_east/2655781.stm

Beaver, R. Pierce, et al., ed. *Eerdmans' Handbook to the World's Religions.* Grand Rapids: Eerdmans, 1983.

Beckwith, Francis. *Baha'i.* Minneapolis: Bethany House, 1985.

Bell, Richard. The *Origin of Islam in Its Christian Environment.* London: Frank Cass and Company, 1968.

Bloom, Jonathan, and Sheila Blair. *Islamic Arts.* London: Phaidon, 1997.

Bosworth, C. E.; E. Van Donzel; B. Lewis; Ch. Pellat, editors. *The Encyclopedia of Islam.* New Edition. Volume V. Leiden: E. J. Brill, 1986.

Braswell, George W. *What You Need to Know about Islam and Muslims.* Nashville: Broadman & Holman, 2000.

Browne, Edward Granville. *A Year Amongst the Persians.* London: Adam and Charles Black, 1926.

Buchanan, Patrick J. "Global resurgence of Islam." *Washington Times.* (August 21, 1989).

Buckner, Jerry L. "Witnessing to the Nation of Islam." *Christian Research Journal.* Vol. 20, No. 3 (January-March 1998), pp. 8,41-2.

Busse, Heribert. *Islam, Judaism, and Christianity: Theological and Historical Affiliations.* Translated by Allison Brown. Princeton: Markus Wiener, 1998.

Bywater, Kevin James. "Is Islam the 'End' of Christianity?" *Christian Research Journal.* Vol. 25, No. 2-3 (2003), pp. 10-1,55; 10-1,53.

Caner, Ergun Mehmet, and Emir Fethi Caner. *Unveiling Islam: An Insider's Look at Muslim Life and Beliefs*. Grand Rapids: Kregel, 2002.

Cares, Mark J. *Speaking the Truth in Love to Mormons*. Milwaukee: WELS Outreach Resources, 1998.

Cofsky, Warren. "Copts Bear the Brunt of Islamic Extremism." *Christianity Today*. (March 8, 1993), pp. 46-7.

Cleary, Thomas, trans. *The Wisdom of the Prophet: Sayings of Muhammad*. Boston & London: Shambhala, 2001.

Coulson, N. J. *A History of Islamic Law*. Edinburgh: Edinburgh University Press, 1964.

Dreher, Rod. "Islam According to Oprah." October 11, 2001. www.national review.com

Duff-Brown, Beth. "Religion figures predominantly in Indian-Pakistani tensions." *Milwaukee Journal Sentinel*. January 6, 2002.

Duiker, William J., and Jackson J. Spielvogel. *World History*. Minneapolis: West, 1994.

Duncan, Randall S. "Muslims Need Jesus." *The Lutheran Witness*. (December 2001), pp. 10-1.

___. "There Is No God but Allah . . ." *The Lutheran Witness*. (March 1995), pp. 6-9.

Dunn, Owen. "The Fatwa on Salman Rushdie." owen@greenend.org.uk

Durant, Will. *The Age of Faith*. Volume 4 in *The Story of Civilization*. New York: Simon and Schuster, 1950.

Esposito, John L. *Islam: The Straight Path*. New York: Oxford University Press, 1988.

___, editor. *The Oxford History of Islam*. Oxford and New York: Oxford University Press, 1999.

The Five Pillars of Islam. Video. Producer and director Michele Arnaud. Princeton, NJ: Films for the Humanities, 1988.

Fromkin, David. *A Peace to End All Peace: The Fall of the Ottoman Empire and the Creation of the Modern Middle East*. New York: Avon Books, 1989.

Fry, C. George, and James R. King. *Islam: A Survey of the Muslim Faith*. Grand Rapids: Baker, 1980.

Fry, C. George. "The Witness of the Cross and the Islamic Crescent." *The Theology of the Cross for the 21st Century*. Edited by Alberto L. Garcia and A. R. Victor Raj. St. Louis: Concordia, 2002.

Geiger, Abraham. *Judaism and Islam*. New York: Ktav Publishing House, 1970.

Geisler, Norman L., and William E. Nix. *A General Introduction to the Bible*. Chicago: Moody Press, 1986.

Gibb, H. A. R., and J. H. Kramers, ed. *Shorter Encyclopedia of Islam*. Ithaca, NY: Cornell University Press, 1961.

Glassé, Cyril. *The New Encyclopedia of Islam*. New York: Alta Mira, 2001.

Glubb, John Bagot. *The Life and Times of Muhammad*. New York: Stein and Day, 1970.

Gonzalez, Justo L. *The Early Church to the Dawn of the Reformation*. Volume 1 in *The Story of Christianity*. San Francisco: Harper & Row, 1984.

Gudel, Joseph P. "Islam Grows into a Strong Presence in America." *Christian Research Journal*. Vol. 23, No. 4 (2001), pp. 6-8.

Guillaume, Alfred. *Islam*. Baltimore: Penguin, 1956.

___. *The Traditions of Islam: An Introduction to Study of the Hadith Literature*. Beirut: Khayats, 1966.

Guthrie, Stan. "Muslim Mission Breakthrough." *Christianity Today*. (December 13, 1993), pp. 20-6.

Hahn, Ernest. *How to Respond to Muslims*. St. Louis: Concordia, 1995.

___. *Why Share Our Faith with Muslims?* St. Louis: Concordia Tract Mission, n. d.

Hamdani, Abbas. "Tradition and Reason in Medieval Islam." Class lectures at the University of Wisconsin-Milwaukee. Spring, 1993.

Heikkinen, Kaye. "The World of Islam: Islamic Civilization and the Middle East." Concordia University, Wisconsin. 1999.

Henry Martyn Institute of Islamic Studies (multiple authorship). *Christian Witness among Muslims*. Bartlesville, OK: Living Sacrifice, 1994.

Hirji-Walji, Hass, and Jaryl Strong. *Escape from Islam*. Wheaton, IL: Tyndale House, 1981.

Hitti, Philip K. *History of the Arabs*. New York: St. Martin's Press, 1970.

Hoerber, Robert G., ed. *Concordia Self-Study Bible: New International Version*. St. Louis: Concordia, 1985.

Hone, William. *The Lost Books of the Bible*. New York: Gramercy, 1979.

Howd, Aimee. "The Other Genocidal War." May 10, 1999. http://user.txcyber.com/~wd5iqr/tcl/sudan.htm

Husain, Ibrahim. *Handbook of Hajj*. Indianapolis: Islamic Teaching Center, 1977.

Ishaq, Ibn. *The Life of Muhammad: Apostle of Allah*. Edited by Michael Edwardes. London: Folio Society, 1964.

"Islam." Brochure from the Royal Embassy of Saudi Arabia Information Office. Washington, D. C., n.d.

Islamic Affairs Department. *Islam: A Global Civilization*. Embassy of Saudi Arabia, Washington, D. C., n.d.

Islamic Mysticism: The Sufi Way. Video. Producer Elda Hartley. Writer Huston Smith. The Mystic's Journey series. Cos Cob, CT: Hartley Film Foundation, 1997.

Jeffery, Arthur, ed. *Materials for the History of the Text of the Qur'an.* Leiden: E. J. Brill, 1937.

___. *A Reader on Islam.* The Hague: Mouton, 1962.

Jenkins, Philip. *Hidden Gospels: How the Search for Jesus Lost Its Way.* Oxford: Oxford University Press, 2001.

Jihad in America. Video. Reporter Steven Emerson. Alexandria, VA: SAE Productions, 1994.

Johnson, Mike. "Qur'an reading assignment stirs passions for and against." *Milwaukee Journal Sentinel.* August 9, 2002.

Kaiser, Walter C., Jr. *The Messiah in the Old Testament.* Grand Rapids: Zondervan, 1995.

Khalifa, Rashad. *Qur'an, Hadith, and Islam.* Fremont, CA: Universal Unity, 2001.

Kritzeck, James. *Anthology of Islamic Literature.* New York: Meridian, 1964.

Kucharsky, David. "Islam: Understanding the New Surge." *Christian Herald.* (February 1981), pp. 51-2,68,70.

Levy, Reuben. *An Introduction to Persian Literature.* New York and London: Columbia University Press, 1969.

Lewis, Bernard. *The Arabs in History.* New York: Harper, 1960.

___. *The World of Islam: Faith, People, Culture.* London: Thames and Hudson, 1976.

Lings, Martin. *Muhammad: His Life Based on the Earliest Sources.* Rochester, VT: Inner Traditions International, 1983.

Lippman, Thomas W. *Understanding Islam: An Introduction to the Muslim World.* Second revised edition. New York: Meridian, 1995.

Livingstone, E. A., ed. *The Oxford Dictionary of the Christian Church.* Third Edition. Oxford and New York: Oxford University Press, 1997.

Lunde, Paul. *Islam.* New York: DK Publishing, 2002.

Luther, Martin. *Appeal for Prayer Against the Turks, 1541.* In *Luther's Works.* Edited by Helmut Lehmann. Vol. 43. Philadelphia: Fortress, 1968. pp. 213-41.

___. *On War Against the Turk, 1529.* In *Luther's Works.* Edited by Helmut Lehmann. Vol.46. Philadelphia: Fortress, 1968. pp. 155-205.

___. *What Luther Says: An Anthology.* Three volumes. Compiled by Ewald M. Plass. St. Louis: Concordia, 1959.

"Ayatollah Khomeini: Man of the Year." *Time.* (January 7, 1980), pp. 8-32.

Maraini, Fosco. *Jerusalem: Rock of Ages.* Translated by Judith Landry. New York: Harcourt, Brace & World, 1969.

Mawdudi, Abul a'la. *An Introduction to the Qur'an.* Montreal: Islamic Circle of North America, 1982.

McDowell, Josh. *Evidence That Demands a Verdict: Historical Evidences for the Christian Faith.* San Bernardino, CA: Here's Life, 1979.

McManners, John, ed. *The Oxford Illustrated History of Christianity.* Oxford and New York: Oxford University Press, 1990.

Miller, G. (Abdulahad Omar). "A Concise Reply to Christianity." Brochure. Peterborough, Ontario: Ordinary Press. 1983.

Miller, Lisa. "Visions of Heaven: How Views of Paradise Inspire—and Inflame—Christians, Muslims and Jews." *Newsweek.* (August 12, 2002), pp. 44-52.

Miller, Roland. "Love Thy Muslim Neighbor." *The Lutheran Witness.* (December 2001), pp. 6-9.

___. *Muslim Friends: Their Faith and Feeling.* St. Louis: Concordia, 1995.

___. "Renaissance of the Muslim Spirit." *Christianity Today.* (November 16, 1979), pp. 16-21.

Miller, William McElwee. *The Baha'i Faith.* Pasadena, CA: William Carey Library, 1974.

___. *My Persian Pilgrimage.* Pasadena, CA: William Carey Library, 1989.

___. *Ten Muslims Meet Christ.* Grand Rapids: Eerdmans, 1969.

Mohammed, Ovey N. *Muslim-Christian Relations: Past, Present, Future.* Maryknoll, NY: Orbis, 1999.

Montecroce, Riccoldo da, and Martin Luther. *Islam in the Crucible: Can It Pass the Test?* Translated by Thomas C. Pfotenhauer. Kearney, NE: Morris, 2002.

Morey, Robert. *The Islamic Invasion: Confronting the World's Fastest Growing Religion.* Eugene, OR: Harvest House, 1992.

Mufausir, Sulaiman. *Jesus in the Qur'an.* Brochure published by the Muslim Students Association. No place or date given.

Muhammad, Amir Nashid. *Muslims in America: Seven Centuries of History (1313-2000).* Beltsville, MD: Amana, 2001.

Netton, Ian Richard. *A Popular Dictionary of Islam.* London: Curzon Press, 1992.

NewsMax. "NYC OKs prayer in School—for Muslims." November 15, 2001. www.newsmax.com/showinsidecover.shtml?a=2001/11/15/74852.

Pache, Rene. *The Inspiration and Authority of Scripture.* Chicago: Moody, 1969.

Parrinder, Geoffrey. *Jesus in the Qur'an.* New York: Barnes & Noble, 1965.

Payne, Robert. *The History of Islam.* New York: Dorset, 1987.

Pelikan, Jaroslav. *The Emergence of the Catholic Tradition (100-600).* Volume 1 in *The Christian Tradition.* Chicago: University of Chicago Press, 1971.

___. *The Spirit of Eastern Christendom (600-1700).* Volume 2 in *The Christian Tradition.* Chicago: University of Chicago Press, 1974.

Pement, Eric. "Louis Farrakhan and the Nation of Islam: Striking a Responsive Chord in the Black Community." *Christian Research Journal.* Vol. 18, No. 4 (Spring 1996), pp. 6-7,44.

Pfander, C. C. *Mizan Ul Haqq.* (The Balance of Truth.) Translated by R. H. Weakley. London: Church Missionary House, 1866.

Pickthall, Muhammad Marmaduke, trans. *The Meaning of the Glorious Qur'an: Text and Explanatory Translation.* Mecca: Muslim World League, 1977.

Polack, W. G. *The Handbook to the Lutheran Hymnal.* St. Louis: Concordia, 1958.

Rahman, Fazlur. *Islam.* Chicago: University of Chicago Press, 1979.

Robinson, Neal. *Christ in Islam and Christianity.* Albany: State University of New York Press, 1991.

Rohde, Marie. "Many different paths lead followers to Islam." *Milwaukee Journal.* February 19, 1995.

Ruthven, Malise. *A Fury for God: The Islamist Attack on America.* London and New York: Granta Books, 2002.

___. *Islam: A Very Short Introduction.* Oxford and New York: Oxford University Press, 1997.

Saal, William J. *Reaching Muslims for Christ.* Chicago: Moody, 1993.

Sahas, Daniel J. *John of Damascus on Islam.* Leiden: E. J. Brill, 1972.

Said, Edward W. *Orientalism.* New York: Vintage Books, 1979.

Salahi, Adil. *Muhammad: Man and Prophet.* New York: Barnes & Noble, 1988.

Saleeb, Abdul, and Norman Geisler. "Understanding and Reaching Muslims." *Christian Research Journal.* Vol. 24, No. 3-4 (2002), pp. 12-21,26-31,45-7.

Shakir, M. H., trans. *The Qur'an.* Elmhurst, NY: Tahrike Tarsile Qur'an, 2002.

Shorrosh, Anis A. *Islam Revealed: A Christian Arab's View of Islam.* Nashville: Thomas Nelson, 1988.

Siddiqi, Muhammad Zubayr. *Hadith Literature: Its Origin, Development and Special Features.* Cambridge: Islamic Texts Society, 1993.

Smith, Henry Preserved. *The Bible and Islam.* New York: Charles Scribner's Sons, 1897.

Tappert, Theodore G., trans. and ed. *The Book of Concord: The Confessions of the Evangelical Lutheran Church.* Philadelphia: Fortress, 1959.

Tucker, Ruth A. *From Jerusalem to Irian Jaya.* Grand Rapids: Zondervan, 1983.

Van Biema, David. "Missionaries under Cover." *Time.* Vol. 161, No. 26 (June 30, 2003), pp. 36-44.

VanDixhoorn, Chad. "Truth Unchanged, Texts Unchanging? The Text of the Bible and the Text of the Qur'an: A Brief History." Unpublished article. Huron College, London, Canada: 1995. www.rim.org/muslim/texts.htm.

Von Grunebaum, G. E. *Classical Islam: A History 600-1258.* Translated by Katherine Watson. New York: Barnes & Noble, 1996.

Waardenburg, Jacques, ed. *Muslim Perceptions of Other Religions: A Historical Survey.* New York and Oxford: Oxford University Press, 1999.

Waines, David. *An Introduction to Islam.* Cambridge: Cambridge University Press, 1995.

Waldman, Steven. "Jesus in Baghdad: Why we should keep Franklin Graham out of Iraq." April 11, 2003. http://slate.msn.com/id/2081432.

Warraq, Ibn, ed. *The Origins of the Koran: Classic Essays on Islam's Holy Book.* Amherst, NY: Prometheus, 1998.

___. *Why I Am Not a Muslim.* Amherst, NY: Prometheus, 1995.

Wendland, Ernst H. "Our Islamic Frontier." *The Northwestern Lutheran.* (February 17, 1980), pp. 54-5.

What Is Ahmadiyyat? Brochure published by the Ahmadiyya Movement in Islam, West Coast Region, n.d.

White, Charles Edward. "Teaching Mark's Gospel to Muslims: Lessons from an African University." *Christianity Today.* (February 8, 1993), pp. 39-40.

White, James R. "Examining Muslim Apologetics: The Bible Versus the Qur'an." *Christian Research Journal.* Vol. 25, No. 3 (2003), pp. 32-41.

Williams, John Alden, ed. *Islam.* New York: George Braziller, 1962.

___. *The Word of Islam.* Austin: University of Austin Press, 1994.

Woodward, Kenneth L. "The Bible and the Qur'an: Searching the Holy Books for Roots of Conflict & Seeds of Reconciliation." *Newsweek.* (February 11, 2002), pp. 50-7.

World Evangelical Alliance. "Saudi Arabia: New Year—Same Challenge." January 2, 2002. www.worldevangelical.org/persecnews.html.

Yeoman, Barry. "The Stealth Crusade." *Mother Jones.* (May-June 2002), pp. 42-9.

Zwemer, Samuel M. *Islam.* New York: Student Volunteer Movement for Foreign Missions, 1907.

Subject Index

Scripture Index